THE ULTIMATE MAN'S SURVIVAL GUIDE TO THE WORKPLACE

THE ULTIMATE MAN'S SURVIVAL GUIDE TO THE WORKPLACE

FRANK MINITER

REGNERY
PUBLISHING
A Division of Salem Media Group

Regnery® is a registered trademark of Salem Communications Holding Corporation

Cataloging-in-Publication data on file with the Library of Congress

ISBN 978-1-62157-791-1
ebook ISBN 978-1-62157-913-7

Published in the United States by
Regnery Publishing
A Division of Salem Media Group
300 New Jersey Ave NW
Washington, DC 20001
www.Regnery.com

Manufactured in the United States of America

10 9 8 7 6 5 4 3 2 1

Books are available in quantity for promotional or premium use. For information on discounts and terms, please visit our website: www.Regnery.com.

For the millions of working Americans who stubbornly get up every morning to keep the lights on, the motors running, the streets clean, the people safe, the children learning ... all the while knowing this is just what good people do.

CONTENTS

INVICTUS

Out of the night that covers me,

Black as the Pit from pole to pole,

I thank whatever gods may be

For my unconquerable soul.

In the fell clutch of circumstance

I have not winced nor cried aloud.

Under the bludgeonings of chance

My head is bloody, but unbowed.

Beyond this place of wrath and tears

Looms but the Horror of the shade,

And yet the menace of the years

Finds, and shall find, me unafraid.

It matters not how strait the gate,

How charged with punishments the scroll.

I am the master of my fate:

I am the captain of my soul.

—WILLIAM ERNEST HENLEY (1888)

INTRODUCTION

THE ULTIMATE MAN'S GUIDE TO THIS #METOO MOMENT

I am devastated that 80 years of my life is at risk of being undermined in the blink of an eye.
—MORGAN FREEMAN[1]

Don't blame former PBS talk show host Charlie Rose, former Fox News host Bill O'Reilly, or former senator and *Saturday Night Live* comedian Al Franken. They aren't responsible for the #MeToo tsunami.

Matt Lauer, the former NBC *Today* show host, didn't give us the sexual-harassment tidal wave either. It wasn't actors Kevin Spacey, Jeremy Piven, Steven Seagal, Arnold Schwarzenegger, Ben Affleck, or Dustin Hoffman. It wasn't former nightly news anchor Tom Brokaw or former CBS chief Leslie Moonves. It wasn't President Donald J. Trump's infamous "locker-room talk" on that 2005 *Access Hollywood* recording. Bill Clinton's alleged rape of Juanita Broaddrick and his alleged sexual assaults of three other women didn't ignite the #MeToo movement—though they should have. Nor was it sparked by accusations of bad behavior against John Bailey, president of the Academy of Motion Picture Arts and Sciences, or Jeff Franklin, creator of Netflix's *Fuller House*, or even the conviction of rapist Bill Cosby.

Former congressman Patrick Meehan of Pennsylvania, once known for his work in Congress fighting against sexual harassment, might have been working with a guilty conscience when he used taxpayer money to settle his own sexual-misconduct complaint, but he didn't start all this either. It also wasn't former Representatives John Conyers of Michigan or Blake Farenthold of Texas, who resigned after sexual harassment charges against them became public.

Ryan Lizza, the *New Yorker*'s former Washington correspondent, was fired over sexual misconduct allegations, but he is hardly the cause of the #MeToo movement. Radio personality Ryan Seacrest isn't to blame. Fashion photographer Patrick Demarchelier isn't the poster boy for this. Wayne Pacelle, former CEO of the Humane Society of the United States, didn't start the flood either, though he did leap right into it.

Former celebrity chef Mario Batali isn't to blame. Nor is Peter Martins, longstanding head of the New York City Ballet. Sexual harassment complaints did knock Garrison Keillor, former host of *A Prairie Home Companion*, off his moral perch, but he isn't to blame. John Lasseter, former chief creative officer of Pixar and Walt Disney Animation Studios went down after a whisper campaign, but his alleged actions didn't start this deluge of sexual harassment complaints either.

Even former film producer Harvey Weinstein isn't to blame for the #MeToo flood, though the allegations against him shook the fault lines of our culture.

If these men are guilty, and some of them surely are, their guilt lies in their individual actions—but they aren't responsible for the cultural crisis behind #MeToo.

So, what is?

Some say the trouble is simply men, or manliness, and that men need to be *weakened* and women need to be *empowered*, though it is not entirely clear what that means.

But if it means men are just *guilty, guilty, guilty* because they are men, then they have little incentive to be part of the solution. And encouraging men to be *weaker* is not a solution when common sense should tell us that we need good, strong men to stand up to bad, powerful ones.

Often missing from the #MeToo conversation is the obvious and critical distinction between the gentlemen who respect women and the obnoxious— and even criminal—few who harass them or worse.

In the media it's just too easy, or too convenient, to condemn an entire sex, to assume that men are inherently bad, and that the "gentleman" is an archaic, irrelevant concept, irrelevant in an age of equality. But is it? Or is this very disdain for the idea of the gentleman what has brought us to the #MeToo crisis?

Being a gentleman is now so misunderstood it is often discouraged. We hear instead about "toxic masculinity." We're told that men are inherently overbearing, abusive, egotistical, even misogynistic. Manliness, in this telling, isn't a virtue; it's a vice.

But manliness, as the gentleman understands it, has nothing to do with these negative qualities. The gentleman is the man of quiet strength who puts others first. He is dedicated to an ideal of service to others. He knows that real strength is a matter of capability, compassion, decency, understanding, stoicism, and self-control, of shouldering responsibility without complaint, of being straightforward, honest, and fair.

These might sound like old-fashioned virtues—but they remain virtues, the sort of virtues that all of America honored when President George H. W. Bush died, an understated war hero, public servant, and dedicated husband, father, and grandfather.

Maybe, just maybe, we need to consider that the "gentleman," as a role model, appeals to the better side of our human nature.

But for skeptics, there remains the question: are the gentleman's rules, his code of conduct, outdated?

My answer is no. Men and women both prosper when men seek to live honorably, courageously, and gallantly. How the rules are applied might change according to circumstances—in that sense, some of the rules *have* changed, but the virtues behind the rules have not.

This book provides the rules a modern gentleman must live by, *especially* today when the innocent as well as the guilty are being swept up by the #MeToo flood. Gentlemanly behavior is not just an ideal, but a neglected necessity in the modern workplace.

RULE 1

UNDERSTAND THE NEW RULES OF THE GAME

[W]hen a woman makes an accusation, the man instantly gets the death penalty. There has to be some sort of due process here. All of these inappropriate behaviors are not all the same.

–GAYLE KING[1]

Your father, or certainly your grandfather, never heard of "toxic masculinity." They didn't have to worry about "microaggressions" (or are they "macroaggressions"?), such as "mansplaining" (talking down to a woman) or "manspreading" (taking up too much space on public transport).

Clearly, the rules have changed. Today you can be deemed "toxic" for simply being manly—you know, strong, stoic, and straightforward.

In hindsight things appear to have been so much simpler for men in the mid-twentieth century. The men who came of age in the 1940s or 1950s or early 1960s could pretty much say what they wanted as long as they didn't use four-letter words in mixed company; for them, sex outside of marriage was frowned upon (which made for clearer boundaries about acceptable and unacceptable behavior) and most people married in their twenties; "gender roles" were assumed to be natural rather than imposed and certainly weren't seen as something that we could change; divorce rates were about half of what they are today; and the illegitimacy rate was about 5 percent compared to 40 percent today (or 70 percent for many minority communities).

Still, things were hardly perfect in 1950s America. The social upheaval in America that began in the 1950s, as people struggled for equality in the civil rights movement, for equal rights for women in the workplace, and for so much more, was partly a necessary reaction to the stringent social conformity of "Leave It to Beaver" America. But revolutions, even necessary social revolutions, often destroy the good along with the bad.

In this case, the effort to upend the "patriarchy" of the American workplace in mid-twentieth-century America didn't stop with expunging real discrimination and other byproducts of sexism and racism. Many in the mainstream media and academia have kept pushing so far that they now think "manliness" needs to be ridiculed and labeled "toxic."

This when the vast majority of men in America today are for #MeToo, as long as it includes due process protections for the accused. Men today don't want workplace monsters preying on their wives, sisters, daughters, and colleagues. They also know that a true egalitarian society was the goal of the women's suffrage movement of the early twentieth century and then of society in general and they aren't just okay with this, they are all for it, as, again, they want their wives, sisters, daughters, and colleagues to have an equal opportunity to advance.

Nevertheless, the pendulum has kept swinging into absurdity. Now a man's strength is viewed by some as being overbearing, overly aggressive, abusive, coldhearted, and even misogynistic. Real strength, of course, means that a man is also compassionate, decent, loving, and understanding, and wants the best for everyone around him; after all, it is harder to be good and compassionate in difficult and stressful circumstances than it is to be an angry, selfish child. Nevertheless, those who now see manliness as toxic don't understand the deeper truth that manly stoicism is self-control.

In time the pendulum will (I am an optimist) swing back to a healthier middle ground that supports real equality and inclusiveness for both sexes. In the meantime, as this is a practical guidebook for men, here are the rules to live by so you won't just survive but will thrive in spite of today's political correctness that so often deems manliness to be "toxic."

Let's begin with twenty-five practical rules for the modern gentleman in today's workplace.

1.   It might sound trite, but it's effective: the first rule is to have a hero, a role model, and to measure your own conduct against his. Most men are competitive and like to measure their achievements against others, so this probably comes naturally. But you must choose your hero wisely, of course, and you'll find some suggestions throughout this book. Evangelical Christians have the catchphrase, "What Would Jesus Do?" But you could choose a historical figure (Abraham Lincoln, Lou Gehrig, Ronald Reagan), or an ideal of masculinity portrayed by an actor (John Wayne, Gary Cooper, Jimmy Stewart), or even, what would *my dad* do? Depending on your father, that might be the best role model of all. But have a hero and follow his example for personal conduct.

2.   Read that employee manual. Yes, it is drivel from lawyers, but you need to be able to quote it back to them.

3.   Eye contact is important. Think about eye discipline. In conversation, a woman will watch a person's eyes; a man will often first look at a person's lips. If you speak with a woman, she'll notice if you sneak a glance anywhere, so don't do it; and if you speak with a man, maintaining eye contact is a sign of confidence.

4.   Always dress a little better than necessary; it'll give you an air of someone who's moving up.

5.   Ear buds are for kids. Ear buds kill conversations and make you seem like you're tuned out.

6.   In the office the tone of your voice should be clear, kind, concise, and never louder than necessary.

7.   Silence your mind and listen, really listen when someone speaks, and respond appropriately. It is really that simple. Many people focus so much on their own thoughts and what they are going to say, that they don't listen—and that's a detriment in any meeting.

8.   Be aware of how posture makes you look: crossed arms are defensive; hands on your hips can be too strong for

some; a slouch or downcast eyes weakens you. Be strong but open and friendly.

9.   Closed-door conversations should be rare and tactfully done. And, in general, a man should not do a closed-door employment review of a woman without another woman present.

10.   Communication in an office quells dissent. If you keep too many work secrets from employees, you will alienate them. Dissension will start. The rumors will be worse than the truth.

11.   You can be diplomatic and honest at the same time. Honesty builds trust; dishonesty destroys it.

12.   Always give credit where it is due.

13.   Demand credit when it is due. (See "When to Demand Credit" for more on this.)

14.   Avoid criticizing others in the office. (But see "When to Speak Badly about a Colleague" for when you must break this rule.)

15.   Be positive and helpful and always ready to do a little more than is required.

16.   Know your company's hierarchy and get clear answers to how you can climb the ladder. Practical, directed ambition is a good thing.

17. Get to know your company's competition. It will make you better in your current job—and might land you another one.

18. Never assume your boss knows what you do for the company. It can be important to quietly assert your authority in areas where you have expertise, but don't overdo it.

19. Never assume that those above you in the company have your best interests at heart. They should, but many won't.

20. Learn: develop new skills; keep up on trends in your business; acquire advanced degrees if necessary; keep yourself versatile, competitive, and valuable to an employer. The challenge of learning new things will make you happier too; you won't feel like you're in a rut.

21. In general, don't text at work. Talk to people face-to-face.

22. Maintain a clean, professional appearance; it shows you care about yourself and those around you.

23. Keep your desk clean and organized. (A man who can't govern himself won't be trusted with supervising others.)

24. The photos in your office are public declarations of who you are—make sure they say the right things.

25. Likewise, social media and the rest of your online profile is your autobiography; make sure it puts your best foot forward.

How a Gentleman Understands Equality in the Workplace

Critics of the gentlemanly ideal say that most men born before the twenty-first century, and all gentlemen, were "sexists." But in truth, the gentleman has a better understanding of equality than modern egalitarians probably do. To a gentleman, "equality" refers to every person's inherent human worth, which is why he is polite and considerate to everyone in the office, from the corporate CEO to the janitorial staff. To the gentleman, equality, in any positive sense, does *not* mean coercing people, dividing people, or imposing quotas to achieve equal, bureaucratically enforced results in achievement, compensation, or the numbers of male and female doctors, engineers, accountants, lawyers, or teachers. The gentleman has too much respect for personal choices and talents to make those judgmental mistakes—and social science backs him up.

Jordan Peterson, the YouTube sensation who is a Canadian clinical psychologist, professor, and author of the bestselling book *12 Rules for Life: An Antidote to Chaos*, points out that Finland, Sweden, and Norway are our best examples of societies that put a premium on achieving male-female equality, yet statistically men and women in those nations have largely segregated themselves into various occupations *by choice*. Peterson's point went viral, with more than fourteen million views on YouTube, when he debated British news personality Cathy Newman on this topic.[2]

Peterson argued that the pay gap that exists between male and female employees is mostly the result of innate differences between men and women, especially on five big personality traits: openness to experience, conscientiousness, extraversion, agreeableness, and neuroticism. In studies of these traits, women consistently report higher neuroticism, agreeableness, warmth (a facet of extraversion), and openness to feelings; whereas men report higher assertiveness (a different facet of extraversion) and openness to ideas. In general, people who score highly on "agreeableness" gravitate to jobs that pay less and that have lesser chances for promotion. On the other hand, people who are "agreeable" are more likely to perform better in many healthcare jobs (especially nursing) and in teaching positions, fields dominated by women.

Peterson told Newman that all the available social science data show that the presumed sexism of employers is only one small factor in the pay gap that exists between men and women. A much bigger factor is biology—the fact that many women become mothers, and mothers, far more than fathers, *choose* to stay home to take care of their young children. If you want to rise to the top of a corporation, taking months or years off work is a disadvantage, but given a choice, many women would rather take time off to be a mother.

Peterson told Newman, "Many women around the age of between 28 and 32 have a career-family crisis that they have to deal with. And I think that's partly because of the foreshortened time-frame that women have to contend with. Women have to get the major pieces of their life put together faster than men."

He cited his work with law firms in Canada where many of the best performers are women, yet many women leave the firms before they can become partners, because they want a better work-life balance.

"Men and women won't sort themselves into the same categories if you leave them alone to do it of their own accord," said Peterson. "We've already seen that in Scandinavia. It's twenty to one female nurses to male...and approximately the same male engineers to female engineers. That's a consequence of the free choice of men and women in the societies that have gone further than any other societies to make gender equality the purpose of the law. Those are ineradicable differences. You can eradicate them with tremendous social pressure and tyranny. But if you leave men and women to make their own choices you will not get equal outcome." [3]

The gentleman's rule is this: treat everyone in the office with equal respect. The real equality that matters is *not* an enforced equality of jobs, salaries, or achievements, but the innate equality of every human being.

How a Man Can Stand Up to Quotas and Other Sexist Policies

When Google engineer James Damore wrote an internal memo saying essentially what Jordan Peterson said—that innate differences between men and women, rather than sexual discrimination, accounted for most of the disparity in the numbers of male and female tech workers—he was fired.

Damore noted that in trying to even up the numbers, Google was in fact discriminating against men. Given that his memo—posted on an internal company discussion board—got him fired, what should he have done? Should he have kept his mouth shut and played along? That is what many or even most men now do—and it is wrong, because nothing good ever came from cowardice.

The real question is not *should* you stand up for yourself but *how*. Damore wasn't protesting a specific instance of sexism on the part of Google. He didn't cite a well-qualified man being passed over for a less-qualified woman by the company. He was articulating a *general* point that ran against the politically correct culture of Google. He was never going to win that argument.

If Damore had protested a specific and provable grievance where he, or someone else in the company, had been discriminated against, he likely could have won his case that he was unjustly fired, and set a precedent. But he started from a weak position. Damore argued he was discussing working conditions and, therefore, his termination was illegal—a claim that the National Labor Relations Board (NLRB) rejected. The NLRB did find that parts of Damore's memo were protected speech, but they determined that Google didn't fire him for that. The NLRB concluded: "[The Employer] determined that certain portions of Damore's memo violated existing policies on harassment and discrimination…."[4] Without a specific grievance, Damore lost the argument—and his job—though his legal battle continues.

Manliness Is Too Often Blamed for What Lawyers Have Done

Blaming men for being men gives a big pass to the legal system, as right now the prevalence of forced arbitration agreements is smothering this #MeToo movement.

Forced arbitration agreements have been deemed legal under contract law by many courts, as they are seen as employment contracts. To invalidate a forced arbitration agreement someone must prove in court that one such agreement fails an arbitrary "unconscionable conduct" test—no easy thing to do.

Still, forced arbitration agreements are very common.

"Among private sector nonunion employees, 56.2 percent are subject to mandatory employment arbitration procedures," reports Workplace Fairness, a nonprofit organization. "Looking at the size of the American workforce, this means that more than 60 million employees no longer have access to the courts in the event they have a workplace related issue."[5]

These legal agreements between corporations and employees keep a lot of complaints out of the newspapers and off cable television. Forced arbitration agreements have thereby suffocated a possible public debate, a debate that would help us understand and address this important issue.

"The institutional answer [to this problem] is to abolish human resources," said S. E. Cupp, host of CNN's *S. E. Cupp: Unfiltered* when interviewed for this book. "When the system for reporting workplace harassment involves informing the entity whose job it is to protect the company, victims lose. Independent and external boards are the only way to ensure victims' safety and continued employment."

Certainly, the first concern of a company's human resources department is to protect the company. This is why so many use forced arbitration agreements to stop employees from going to the legal system for a remedy. The trouble is this can put employees dealing with a bad CEO or other person in a senior leadership position at a disadvantage, which is a big reason why so many actors and CEOs who might have been preying on the people they employed were able to get away with all they allegedly did for so long.

Congress has also used administrative procedures to hush up staffers who've accused members of Congress of sexual harassment. Members of Congress even used a slush fund (taxpayer money) to pay victims for silence. Clearly, the bureaucracy and the legal tools used by corporations today are part of the reason why so many #MeToo complaints have been silenced in America.

This legalistic climate has made not acting by far the safer option in almost every case. Action today is often punished. Even courageous government whistleblowers often get destroyed by the bureaucracy they speak up to cleanse. Not acting, in contrast, is rarely punished. You almost have to be an eyewitness to a rape who walked away without saying anything to realize consequences later. Even then in today's legal climate you could get off by simply saying you were too traumatized to act. In these ways our legalistic society has created disincentives to be manly, to be men of action who do what's right despite the potential costs.

Learning When to Deflect Harassment and When to Intervene Against It

When I was a twenty-five-year-old young man working for a magazine in Manhattan, I was power-harassed by an older woman who was in a management position. There was no easy way out of the uncomfortable situation. She did all she could to belittle me. I opted to confront her with humor and decency until she backed off. It took several months. I later defended her publicly when she was harassed by someone in the office. She ended up being a good mentor and we are still friends. So never assume that an office conflict can't be resolved graciously.

But, of course, sometimes it can't. I recall an office creep who regularly phone-harassed a woman in the office. The woman declined to make a complaint. She didn't want to be known as an office tattler. Her manager (a gentleman) offered to take the matter up with human resources, but she didn't want him to do that. At the time I thought, *Well, that's her decision.* Her manager quietly told the creep to stop phoning her, and he did. But her manager's decision, however well intentioned, turned out to be a mistake, because the creep went on to harass other women until he was fired for related, but different reasons. The manager, as I noted, was a gentleman, but a gentleman needs to know when a quiet word isn't enough, and when he needs to play corporate hardball. He should have reported the incident to human resources. As a manager, that was his job.

I could deflect the harassment directed against me, because the manager involved eventually understood that she had overstepped her bounds. Aggressive managers can sometimes do this, and a polite reminder can make them dial it back. But the creep was in a different category. He wasn't going to be dissuaded until he was fired, and corporate human resources, which puts a premium on protecting a company's reputation, should have been alerted immediately.

Don't Be Guilty of These Bad Workplace Habits

For both managers and employees, the golden rule—*Do unto others as you would have them do unto you*—is still good policy, maybe more so now than ever. The issue is not just avoiding harassment; it's avoiding the problem of *proximity* in the modern office.

Many companies today stuff their employees into cubicles or even along open tables. The noises you make, the food you eat, all the things you do in the course of an ordinary business day will have an impact on those around you.

Gentlemanly behavior is paramount in these new office environments. It's basic, and something you probably should have learned in kindergarten, but you would be amazed how many people need reminders. Here are a few.

1. **Don't make a lot of noise.** This is nearly every employee's pet peeve—the office noisemaker. Your colleagues don't expect silence all the time—that would be eerie—but loud phone conversations (or conference calls; hint: use a headset), singing or playing the radio at your desk (it happens), or otherwise disregarding those around you is a no-no.

2. **Be careful about bringing spicy or odiferous food to work.** Your colleagues might not appreciate it. Save your Mexican, Indian, or Thai food for dinner at home.

3. **Don't delay work with excessive small talk.** When you speak, be concise. Time, as they say, is money, and good employees want to be efficient.

4. **It is astonishing how many people ignore the most basic rules of manners.** It should go without saying, but it doesn't: you should not bite (or trim) your nails or pick (or floss) your teeth in the office or on your commute into work. Don't do anything in public that would embarrass you if it was posted online (because someday it might be).

5. **If you are so sick that you cannot stop coughing and sneezing, take a sick day and stay home.** Gentlemen used to carry handkerchiefs, but also rarely used them,

When to Demand Credit

If you're bothered by not getting your due, speak up, but do it respectfully and privately; and if you're rebuked you will learn an important thing about the quality of your manager—and maybe whether you should begin looking for a new job.

and that should be your guideline. If you expect you'll need an entire packet of Kleenexes to get through the day, your colleagues probably don't want you at the office.

6.   **Don't be a touchy-feely type.** It easily crosses the line into annoyance or sexual harassment, as even touchy-feely politicians like Joe Biden have learned.

7.   **Don't invade others' space.** No matter how cramped your office, everyone has their territory. Respect it.

8.   **Don't be moody.** When you are in the office you have a job to do—so do it. Don't inflict your emotions on your colleagues.

When to Speak Badly about a Colleague

Outside of a performance review, the general rule is never.

For the most part, you should be stoic if you have a bad-mannered, ill-tempered, or incompetent boss, manager, or fellow employee. Don't stoop to their level. Try to make them rise to yours.

But there are exceptions; there are times when you need to do more than set a positive example.

If, for instance, someone is doing something criminal, you need to report it. You can be held legally responsible if you look the other way when a colleague or even a superior commits theft, fraud, assault, or sexual harassment. More than that, you need to be able to live with yourself—and that means confronting evil when you see it.

I once interviewed a U.S. Army nurse who told me how Afghan soldiers rounded up boys for "*bacha bazi,*" an Afghan term for pederasty. She was told, as American soldiers were told, to stay in the barracks and ignore the boys' screaming as they were raped; this was part of Afghan culture and Americans were not to interfere. She followed her orders and suffers post-traumatic stress disorder as a result. That's an extreme example, but we'd all rather be the hero

How to Survive an Office Witch Hunt

Be wary of contributing to office gossip. You don't have to close your ears—it's fine to be tuned in to what other employers are saying—but don't offer additional gossip or opinion, and don't repeat what you hear. That's the most honorable way to navigate office storms. You need to protect yourself, because you cannot assume that managers or bosses will be fair. Too often they will make decisions based on expediency and self-protection, and you don't want to inadvertently put yourself at hazard.

than the guy who looked the other way—and in the office and in our neighborhoods we should be.

The Truth about "Toxic Masculinity" in the Workplace

When it comes to so-called "toxic masculinity," the best advice is to forget about it, or dismiss it as an absurdity. Neither one sex nor the other is toxic, and a true gentleman brings masculine *virtues* to the office that everyone can value. Here are a few that you should put into practice.

1.   **Resiliency.** Every man who has played sports when he was young has had a coach tell him to "shake it off" when he got injured. Businesses need employees who know that a setback or a challenge is something to be overcome.

2.   **Risk-taking.** Not all risks are worth taking, of course, but no one ever launched a business without a willingness to roll the dice.

3.   **Competitiveness.** Most men love sports because they love competition, but the gentleman knows that competitions have rules, so he never lets his desire to compete, succeed, and win in the business world overwhelm his belief in treating people with consideration and respect. He's never guilty of what NFL referees call "unsportsmanlike conduct." He believes in playing the game hard, but in the right way.

4.   **Self-reliance.** Okay, a business is a cooperative venture, but every manager values the employee who can manage

himself, take the initiative, and get things right done without needing constant supervision.

5. **Strength and Courage.** It's not just physical strength and courage that matters in a man, it is the moral strength and courage to do what is right—and in business that sometimes means protecting good employees from bad ones.

Bottom line: there is no such thing as toxic masculinity. There are only good men and bad men. We need more of the former—and reviving the ideal of the gentleman is a big part of that.

What Is Toxic: Sexual Harassment

Legally, sexual harassment describes unwelcome sexual advances or offensive remarks about a person's sex, but there are plenty of gray areas, in part because of changing moral standards—and by that I don't mean that moral standards are getting better; in fact, the explosion of sexual harassment cases would indicate that they have gotten worse.

The U.S. Equal Employment Opportunity Commission defines sexual harassment this way:

> It is unlawful to harass a person (an applicant or employee) because of that person's sex. Harassment can include "sexual harassment" or unwelcome sexual advances, requests for sexual favors, and other verbal or physical harassment of a sexual nature. Harassment does not have to be of a sexual nature, however, and can include offensive remarks about a person's sex. For example, it is illegal to harass a woman by making offensive comments about women in general.

Advice from the Office Gentleman
Good men do not superficially judge others, but only try to understand them. Conversely, a stand-up man does not care how others judge him.

21

Both victim and the harasser can be either a woman or a man, and the victim and harasser can be the same sex. Although the law doesn't prohibit simple teasing, offhand comments, or isolated incidents that are not very serious, harassment is illegal when it is so frequent or severe that it creates a hostile or offensive work environment or when it results in an adverse employment decision (such as the victim being fired or demoted). The harasser can be the victim's supervisor, a supervisor in another area, a co-worker, or someone who is not an employee of the employer, such as a client or customer.[6]

That covers a lot of ground but doesn't give much useful advice. So here's a rule of thumb from the office gentleman: When you're in the office, speak and behave as if your mother, wife, or daughter were listening. That way you won't say anything inappropriate—unless your mother was someone like Rosie O'Donnell.

Let Mentors Teach the Rules

It is hip for new hires to seek out a mentor; many companies even assign them to young employees. Be wary though; while a good mentor can be a useful guide, a bad one might take you across the River Styx.

As a journalist, I always seek mentors—experts who can help me with whatever I'm assigned to write about. For instance, before I ran with the bulls in Spain's San Fermín Fiesta, I found Juan Macho—someone who had not only run with bulls there and elsewhere, more than a hundred times in all, but who could tell me more than I could ever have discovered on my own about how what started as a means to drive bulls to market became a wild and dangerous competition, and then an integral part of a Catholic celebration.

Having a guide like that can be invaluable. The history of your company is likely not so deep, but there is still a lot to learn in any job—not just the technical aspects, though those can be overwhelming enough, but the culture of a company, its hierarchy, and the personalities and expectations that drive it. Finding the right mentor can put you on the fast track to success within a company. But be wary of the mentor who takes you aside and tells you how to *work the system*. He'll either get you in trouble in the end, or he'll be revealing a toxic workplace from which you'll want to escape.

Three Prominent Women on How Men Can Still Be Men in the Workplace

Besides having a good mentor, we should know, as gentlemen, what women in the workplace expect of us. A story on Bloomberg.com highlighted one unintentional effect of the #MeToo movement. It was headlined: "Wall Street Rule for the #MeToo Era: Avoid Women at All Cost."[7] Obviously, no one benefits from that, but that's where hysteria, hypersensitivity, and lawyers are driving us. Still, it doesn't have to be that way. I asked three prominent women, respected commentators well known in media circles, about how to bring some sanity back into a business world that is struggling to come up with new rules to govern its employees. I got some surprising answers.

Heather Mac Donald is an essayist and bestselling author, most recently of *The Diversity Delusion: How Race and Gender Pandering Corrupt the University and Undermine Our Culture*. I asked her how a businessman should conduct himself to avoid any potential trouble with female colleagues. She told me that "The most risk-averse stance" a man can take "in today's #MeToo frenzied corporate work environment" would be to try to ignore "female sexuality and attractiveness" entirely and see male and female coworkers "as fungible components of the workplace." But, she added, that's not very likely. So, in practice, the safest thing to do is to "avoid any testing of mutual interest and any possible reference to sexual humor. The Mike Pence rule [of avoiding being alone with any woman who isn't your wife] seems eminently reasonable. Obviously, feminists want it both ways…[they] lambasted Pence for being a prude and denying females networking opportunities."

ERNEST HEMINGWAY

(1899–1961)

When people talk, listen completely.

—ERNEST HEMINGWAY

Ernest Hemingway was a man of strength and bravery who lived by a deeply masculine code that he expressed in his life and in his literary art. He was wounded while serving as an ambulance driver in World War I, and he eventually came to Paris, where he lived with his first wife, Hadley. He worked as correspondent for the *Toronto Star*, but when he found journalism was getting in the way of his desire to write short stories and novels, he dropped journalism. Journalism had shaped his literary style, but so too had the paintings of the French impressionists. He wrote later about how his view of their paintings "sharpened" when he was "belly-empty, hollow-hungry," or in other words, how financial sacrifice had tightened his focus on artistic design and ambition. He noted, in his posthumously published *A Moveable Feast*, "I learned to understand Cezanne much better and to see truly how he made landscapes when I was hungry."[8] Quitting his job was a modest risk—his wife had a small financial trust they could live on—but Hemingway took it to follow the artist's path.

When in Paris he became friends with F. Scott Fitzgerald, who wrote beautiful, poetic prose. Hemingway studied Fitzger-ald's *The Great Gatsby* before beginning his first novel *The Sun Also Rises*. Though Hemingway thought *Gatsby* grand, and told Fitzgerald so, he modeled his own simple, direct style on trying to achieve in words what artists like Paul Cézanne achieved with a paint brush. He wanted to redirect American literature into something simpler, yet more profound. He rejected old-world literary romanticism and gave the novel, as a literary form, a cleaner more direct voice with gritty, real characters. His prose reads so simply it can be difficult to untangle why it is so beautiful.

Though their styles were very different, Fitzgerald helped Hemingway. He even introduced Hemingway to his editor at Charles Scribner's Sons. But Hemingway nevertheless was his own man and could be penetrating in his criticism, even of his friends. Of Fitzgerald, he said, "His talent was as natural as the pattern that was made by the dust on a butterfly's wings. At one time he understood it no more than the butterfly did and he did not know when it was brushed or marred. Later he became conscious of his damaged wings and of their construction and he learned to think and could not fly anymore because the love of flight was gone and he could only re-member when it had been effortless."[9]

Hemingway certainly had his flaws. He drank, smoke, and swore—and though he tried to do it at the proper times and in the right proportion, he didn't always succeed. He was arguably an alcoholic for much of his life. He was married four times. He cheated on some of his wives. Occasionally, he lived off their money. But he also tried to compen-sate for his flaws. After he left his first wife, Hadley, with their young son, he gave her all the royalties from his novel *The Sun Also Rises*—a tidy sum as it turned out. He con-verted to Catholicism, because he believed it to be true, but also because he thought it would make him a better man.

Hemingway was a man of many parts. He liked guns and hunting and fishing, but he also read prodigiously and wrote elegant prose. He loved a refined drink, collected fine art, and had traveled the world, but he also enjoyed boxing. He mocked the "café trash" in Paris, but he also mingled with them and was drawn to those who were honestly trying to be painters and writers and not just posing as artists. He lived his life with gusto—at war, on safari, at sea—and bragged of his brushes with death, but killed himself, probably as a result of clinical depression that could be treated today.

Hemingway's code favored those who lived boldly and honestly. In *Death in the Afternoon* (1932), he asks: "You went to the bullfight? How was it?" One person answers "disgusting" and Hemingway gives him an "honorable discharge." Another says "ter-rible" and gets the same pass. But then one says, "I was simply bored to death." Heming-way says, "All right. You get the hell out of here."[10] His reaction is simple: if your eyes are open and you are honest, you're all right, but if you are sleepwalking through life, or hiding behind a false front, or too shallow to appre-ciate the world in front of you, you'd better get the hell away. He appreciated honesty, he appreciated work, and he appreciated men who lived by a masculine code that governed their behavior—all of which were reasons that he respected bullfighters, men who pol-ished their craft and lived by strict rules of conduct.

There is much more to say about Heming-way, of course, but the point is he wasn't just a maverick or an artist or an egotist. He was all those things, at least in part, but he also made a lifelong effort to understand himself, his art, and the world around him. Open eyes, an understanding mind, and a strong view of yourself are what it takes to chart your own way in today's workplace, whether you're at the bottom rung of a small company, work-ing at a Fortune 500, or embarking on your own start-up. Whatever course you follow should be undertaken as an adventure. And it should be lived like a man, which means being guided by a strict moral code that will give you self-respect and provide the guard-rails as you traverse this #MeToo era.

She noted that men are increasingly reluctant to be mentors to women in the workplace, because they fear potential lawsuits. She commented that not only is this "completely understandable" but that feminists need to come up with a way to guarantee such mentors immunity. "If they can't, it is reasonable for a male to decline such mentorship."

S. E. Cupp, the host of CNN's *S. E. Cupp: Unfiltered*, has herself been subjected to sexual harassment, but she thinks that "singling out the problem of workplace sexual harassment with young men just creates a culture of fear, paranoia, division, and possibly even resentment. All of that is ultimately bad for men and bad for women. I don't want men to be afraid of us or to wall themselves off from us to protect themselves. Young men should be taught to respect everyone—people who look different, who are differently abled, who have different political views, and, of course, women. Abusing one's position or status is never right, and neither is exploiting the vulnerable. Acknowledging that men and women are different is important. We see the world in different ways, have different experiences and different biology. That doesn't make masculinity toxic, nor should we be persuading men to 'act more like women.' But empathy is a language we can all learn. We should look more at behavior—disrespect, bullying, abuse—that is bad no matter who's doing it."

Carrie Lukas, president of the Independent Women's Forum went even further, telling me that "The demonization of masculinity and males in general is profoundly unhelpful—it hurts men as well as women. Teaching boys and men that there is something inherently wrong with themselves can only breed resentment."

She noted the hypocrisy of a media and academic establishment that allegedly opposes male and female stereotypes and sees "gender as a spectrum" but at the same time is pushing "to stereotype boys and men…in the worst possible way."

"It should go without saying," she added, "that we should treat everyone… as an individual deserving of respect. And we should appreciate the positive characteristics that we associate with maleness. Male strength and bravery put to good use has been and will always be critical to women's well-being and advancement."

Heather Mac Donald seemed pessimistic that feminists would concede that point, telling me that "We are seeing a feminist revolt against male civilization *tout court*" and an environment in which inevitable office flirtations "are translated into instances of predatory harassment that can get a male fired."

Like Lukas, Mac Donald pins some of the blame on the media. "The media is not addressing the issue fairly. It is on a feminist crusade to demonize men and to engineer at least 50-50 parity in management."

S. E. Cupp thinks the media has done a better job than that. "Largely, I think the media has given the issue its appropriate spotlight and a good amount of coverage. Most have struck an important balance, refusing to cover for or justify bad behavior while avoiding maligning all men. On a macro level, I [give] the media an A. But while we've done a good job spotlighting the celebrity and mogul cases of sexual harassment, we've done a worse job spotlighting systemic abuse in less glamorous industries. What's sexual harassment like in manufacturing, hospitality and public education? What does the restaurant worker, truck stop waitress and salesperson experience? Local news is good at these sorts of deep dives. I'd like to see more of them."

Carrie Lukas says there is no reason to think that sexual harassment is worse now than it was before. "Certainly everyone—men and women—are more aware that there can be legal consequences to bad behavior than there were in earlier generations. However, our culture has gotten much coarser than it used to be—profanity and sexual content is everywhere, which may contribute to confusion about what is, and what's not, appropriate. Years ago, people could rehash favorite TV shows and feel comfortable that it was appropriate for everyone. But now our most common culture is replete with what used to be considered out of bounds. This makes it much less black and white about what is appropriate in public."

S. E. Cupp told me that while the "majority of men are decent, thoughtful, and respectful," sexual harassment is nevertheless "a problem in a majority of

American workplaces…and men are often victims too. The abuse of power in the workplace is real, not invented or imagined or exaggerated." Cupp adds that "the best way to change a climate that protects sexual harassers is for men and women to say something when they see something. A common thread in all of the #MeToo stories is how many people knew."

Lukas said the most important thing is to keep a sense of perspective and "to restore an appreciation for degrees of behavior. Someone telling an inappropriate joke or asking someone out on a date isn't harassment. We need to reserve allegations and accusations for real wrongdoing. I don't want my sons to have to feel like they are constantly under the threat of an accusation when they haven't done anything wrong—though today, I would definitely tell a young man that he should recognize that he cannot be certain that, in the court of public opinion at least, he will be presumed innocent and needs to be very careful about whom he surrounds himself with."

Lukas added, "I have two young sons, and when they get older I'll tell them that they should always err on the side of caution. It's a little sad, but the stakes are so high that I would prefer that they are on guard when talking with coworkers, male and female, but especially female. I'll tell them of the adage that you shouldn't do or say anything that you wouldn't want on the front page of a newspaper." And, she told me, she would "point to role models that they know in our family and communities—their father, uncles, and grandfathers, and their coaches and teachers. I'm fortunate that the men they come in contact with are almost without exception models of kindness to women and everyone."

RULE 2

A MAN'S IMAGE MUST NOT BE A WORK OF FICTION

A man's face is his autobiography. A woman's face is her work of fiction.
—OSCAR WILDE, *Impressions of America*

A man should be what he seems.

If you have to hide a big part of yourself at work or at home then something is wrong, and you need to fix it.

This is a rule because a man can't be his best if he must hide much of who he is. We cannot be Bruce Wayne and Batman. Both roles suffer in any nonfiction life. This isn't to say we can't quietly be heroes; actually, being truly heroic means being humble, and therefore quiet about our gallantry. What this means is we can't play different characters with different values and expect one not to bleed on the other.

We excel when we're the same honest person at work as we are during our off hours. Superman can be nerdy and wimpy Clark Kent before whirling into the caped hero in red and blue at the first hint of calamity, but he wasn't even human in fiction. He is from the imaginary planet Krypton.

All of us have seen someone who hates their job and so transforms themselves behind a mask of indifference as they enter their workplace. They become unhappy shadows of themselves. They are not as productive as they could be because they are not fulfilled. They are not likeable because they are deeply unhappy. Their chance of getting a promotion plummets because of their attitude. As they get older, they'll likely submit and become half-dead employees, the walking dead of the American workplace. Or maybe they'll finally get fired—no one likes someone who deadens the life of a workplace—and then they might really get bitter. Or perhaps something in them will grow and grow until they finally rebel and quit. They'll have a chance to become something then if they already haven't given up too much.

Now think about the happiest people you know. Chances are, they are comfortable in their skins. They fit in with their surroundings, colleagues, and friends. They have youthful enthusiasm, even if they are not young. They are what they seem. They don't change if they've had a few drinks after hours, because they are who they are. They having nothing to hide, and they treat others with dignity, strength, and respect. You like them, because you feel you know them and can trust them. They get promoted. People like working for them. True, some resent their comfort and happiness—but those who do are mostly the employees that don't fit in, who hate their jobs, who are deeply unhappy, who are insincere when they are nice and backbiting whenever they can. These are the bitter walking dead of the American workforce. They didn't change course—in their careers or in their development of character or personality—when they should have.

If you are not where you want to be, you need to do an honest self-assessment and figure out how to get there. Maybe it means switching companies or careers. Maybe it means finding a better mentor. Maybe it means enlarging or diversifying your skills. Maybe it means an attitude adjustment—and doing the things that give you hope, because from hope comes happiness. Sometimes that means digging deep into our interior lives and confronting things about ourselves that need to change. Success, as the world often measures it—in terms of money or fame—is no guarantee of happiness. It is the journey that counts. It is the journey you choose. And you should choose the heroic part. That choice makes all the difference. That doesn't mean you have to be a superhero. It does mean that you should be humble, honest, and strong—a gentleman.

And that's exactly what the #MeToo villains are not. They practice deception, because they know what they are doing is wrong. They hide their own insecurities, unhappiness, and failings by belittling others, which is what their abuse of women (or men) is all about—making themselves feel important by demeaning someone else, by using people purely for personal, often perverted, gratification.

If, however, you're a stand-up man of honor and action and honestly show people this, well then you'll be liked, successful, comfortable in your role, and forever moving up to greater quests. It still won't be easy. And you'll still be guilty of being a man in this contradictory age, but no one is perfect.

Image Isn't Everything, Just the First Thing

Let's be clear: being what you seem doesn't mean showing up at work as the unshaven mess you were at six in the morning, because that's not what a

> **"All the world's a stage, and all the men and women merely players: they have their exits and their entrances; and one man in his time plays many parts, his acts being seven ages."**
>
> WILLIAM SHAKESPEARE, *AS YOU LIKE IT*, ACT II, SCENE VII

gentleman is. A gentleman is a man who is not only himself, but a man who puts others at ease, who makes others feel comfortable, and a big part of that is manners, and dressing and behaving appropriately; it is taking pains to do things right. How you dress, how you behave, and what you say becomes who you are—in fact, it's one way to become the man you want to be.

If you want to be a doctor, how well you wear your white coat, how you behave, the words you use are what can separate the kindly doctor with a bedside manner that inspires confidence and trust from the perhaps equally well-trained but sloppy, awkward, and curt doctor whose bedside manner inspires doubt and even fear. You need to remember, too, that choosing one route means not choosing another. If you're interested in medicine but decide you're hopeless with people, then perhaps you'd be better off as a medical researcher.

If you see a tie as a leash that empowers corporate America to drag you around and make you sit where it pleases, then you don't belong in a workplace that demands you wear a suit and tie. If you find it embarrassing or belittling to be in a janitor's overalls, then that occupation is not for you. This isn't to say that you should quit and starve. A man does what he must to feed his family. But it does mean you should be in night school or whatever else it will take to get you out of the role that is eating away at you. You need hope. You need to climb out of your despair and if the doors aren't open to you, you must open a window; if the windows are all barred, you must make your own doorway.

Along the way, remember that image isn't everything, just the first thing. If you want to reach the next floor, you must look the part. If, however, you must wear a costume that doesn't fit to try to make it to the top floor then people will notice, as you won't feel comfortable in the role. So before you ask for something, including a promotion, ask yourself what you want and talk to others to get better information about what's really beyond the next door.

Playing parts that fit you in each chapter of your life, now that's the good stuff.

You Are What You Are Online

Do you want to be defined as that guy in the photo shotgunning a beer at a frat house? How about that guy posing with the dead deer? Sure, both might be you, but do they completely define you? Probably not, but anything that's posted online can be—and, if you have enemies, will be—taken out of context. So, don't post anything that could be misconstrued. A photo once tagged on Facebook can turn up in Google searches of you forever.

What Women See in Your Profile

Elizabeth Kantor, author of *The Jane Austen Guide to Happily Ever After*, once told me she doesn't trust a man she can't find much about online. This surprised me, as I have always been cautious about putting too much of my personal life out there. When I pushed back, she said, "Well, I suppose some older men aren't comfortable with being open on social media." I am in my forties. I got my first email address in 1993 when I was a freshman in college, so I don't consider myself a technophobe.

Still, though I don't think she is completely right (reticence is a male virtue, and many good men I know don't like to talk about themselves period, and online especially), her perspective is revealing. Women will Google you. They will look over your social media. They will appreciate finding out who you are—so what you have posted better represent who you really are at your best.

Manage Online Photos

A good rule of thumb is not to post anything you wouldn't want your mother to see. Remember that a photo that might seem funny at the time might not seem funny in the cold light of the morning—or a year or two or three later, when it could cost you (or a buddy) a job or a relationship.

A Man's Online Profile Needs These Accoutrements

An online profile—or all that is publicly searchable about you—shouldn't be so empty that it seems like you're hiding big dark secrets. You can round out your story with video posts that highlight your interests (like, say, skiing); photos that show you hard at work are usually not a bad idea; and blogs that highlight intellectual interests (anything from mathematics to viticulture) can illustrate a bit of your depth. Things to avoid—or to be extremely cautious about—are online comments on other posts, likes, and online "friends." There is guilt by association in life and online. Don't just click yes on everyone who wants to be your friend. Choose your friends wisely. Be careful about who and what you like, and remember that every comment can be turned against you if it is sophomoric, controversial, or could be taken out of context. Ideally, your online profile should be your professional portfolio. Other people will certainly regard it as such. Employers routinely look for more information on potential employees by Googling their names.

The Well-Thought-Out Entrance

Let's get offline now, and back in the real world. Here, too, first impressions count—and that means something as simple as how you enter a room.

Women think about their entrances much more than men typically do. Women often think about how they walk, about their posture, about the movement of their hands, about how they'll sit (both feet on the floor or legs crossed).

Men often just stupidly stumble in and figure they can handle it—whatever it is, a business meeting or a date. This approach has its merits, as it can broadcast simple, unscripted confidence. It also has its downsides, as it can leave a man unprepared for the scene in which he needs to play a starring role.

The best way to create a good entrance is to visualize the place you'll be—an office, a restaurant—and you in the scene. See yourself moving confidently with your shoulders back, a strong stride, and a confident smile on your face. Once you've established yourself, be aware of your surroundings and whoever it is you're talking to, and be prepared to listen and respond thoughtfully.

Here are the fundamentals for different situations.

The Pickup: The big mistake is the too-practiced line, or lines, which you'll forget or stumble over in the heat of the moment, *and not listening.* Stay calm, make eye contact, and when you introduce yourself don't stand too close, so that you don't appear too eager or intimidating. Listen and respond, with light humor if possible. If she doesn't seem interested in talking with you, politely move on.

The Date: She is there to see you. So enter confidently, but take yourself lightly. Turn the conversation to her, let her know you're interested in what she thinks, but don't interrogate her. She'll tell you—in her words or in her manner—if she's interested in another date.

The Interview: You need to look the part—again, if the part is not you, you are in the wrong interview. Be clean and on time, courteous and confident. Don't lie, not about anything. I once didn't get a job because I lied about something that I thought didn't matter. I interviewed for a summer position while I was in college, and the interviewer asked if I had another job. I said, "No," because I wanted the interviewer to know I was wide-open to doing whatever needed to be done on this job. But I found out later that he already knew about the other job, and passed me over because he felt he couldn't trust me. That taught me an important lesson: always, *always* tell the truth, even about things that seem trivial. That does not mean, of course, that you treat an interview as a confessional. Just be honest and truthful. The best defense is to live your life prudently, honorably, and well.

Shake hands when you enter—grip the other person's hand firmly, shake it once, maintain eye contact, and smile; that's it—and then sit with your back straight. Make sure your cell phone is switched to silent mode. Fill any awkward pauses with compliments about the office or the potential employer.

Advice from the Office Gentleman
Don't slouch. Keep your shoulders back and look others in the eyes with friendly confidence.

The Business Meeting: Other than your appearance and entrance, realize this isn't all about you. You are there to forge a transaction that will be mutually beneficial; the best salesman knows he is there to help his potential client. Focus on service; money can come later.

One businessman I know who owns an import/export company won't even talk money in a business meeting. He waits until he's at the airport. He makes great deals because he concentrates on building a relationship and providing great service. Maybe even more important, he is incorruptible. He has turned down countless illicit payoffs, which has built him a sterling reputation for integrity and won him enormous trust from his clients.

The Ultimate Posture of a Man

Your body language broadcasts a message, so it's important to position yourself in a way that's strong, open, and confident. Here are some tips.

1. Whether standing or sitting, keep your back straight but not stiff (one trick is to lean back slightly) and let your shoulders relax (no shrugging). You want to look attentive and comfortable.

2. Establish your space. Stand or sit with your legs apart a bit. You'll look more at ease with yourself and less like someone who's afraid to be noticed.

3. When someone is talking in a meeting, it can be a good idea to lean slightly towards the speaker; it shows you're paying close attention.

4. Hands on hips broadcasts impatience; crossing your arms is defensive; hands together near your lap is a

listening posture. Make sure your body language fits the situation.

5.   Eye contact is very important, but make sure your look is one of friendly attentiveness and you are not staring. Like all good rules, this one can be broken to great effect. Spencer Tracy demolished Robert Ryan in the 1955 film *Bad Day at Black Rock* by looking at the ground as he responded to Ryan's threats. Doing that isn't easy, but it made for a great scene. Study it, if you want to emulate it.

6.   When someone else is talking, nodding your head and smiling appropriately are important—it helps put the speaker at ease.

7.   When you speak, remember to slow down. Almost all of us speak much faster than we realize. You'll come across as more contemplative and articulate if you slow down.

> " Clothes make the man. Naked people have little or no influence in society. "
>
> MARK TWAIN[1]

How a Man Moves

A man moves with purpose and simplicity, but that doesn't mean the way you move can't be distinctive. John Wayne always moved with purpose, and his definitive walk—parodied wonderfully by actor Nathan Lane in the movie *The Birdcage* (1996)—naturally suited his frame and character. It wasn't strutting, and its inherent swagger fit the man. Make sure your walk fits you. You can set a fast, determined pace, as a man who gets things done, or you can follow the relaxed, ambling pace of a man with time for everything and everyone. It's all up to what you need to do and the image, true to yourself, that you want to convey.

How to Dress Like a Gentleman

Gentlemanly behavior is not won or lost by the cut, fit, and style of a man's suit, but that is where it begins. A good suit is a presentation of how seriously you take yourself and want to be taken by others. That's why a man's suit—conservative by design—can be debonair and dashing, strong and elegant. The goal of a good suit is to make you look good, but not slick. It should be handsome and well-crafted, but not something from the "luxury menswear boutique." The idea is to put your best foot forward, but naturally, not in a self-conscious or showy way.

One of George Washington's *Rules of Civility & Decent Behavior* was: "Play not the peacock, looking everywhere about you to see if you are well decked, if your shoes fit well, if your stockings fit neatly, and your clothes handsomely." Instead of playing the peacock, Washington always presented a dignified appearance, respectable, well kept, but not ostentatious.

The Shirt

The dress shirt hasn't changed much since the early twentieth century, when a breast pocket was added (for holding reading glasses) after the three-piece suit (with vest) went out of fashion (though traditional shirts have never adopted the breast pocket).

Here are some things to look for in a quality shirt.

Buttons: Poorly sewn on buttons are a giveaway sign of a poorly made shirt. For traditionalists, buttons should be made of mother-of-pearl (nacre), a substance so hard it can crack needles.

Gusset: Good shirts typically have a triangular piece of material added to reinforce the side seam of a shirt.

Pleated sleeves: On a quality shirt the material on the sleeve is pleated several times where it is stitched into the cuff. There is also typically a small button above the cuff to prevent it from opening and showing the forearm.

Where patterns meet: On good shirts all the patterns or lines should meet up properly. On cheap shirts the patterns are often out of alignment.

Stitches: The stitches on a shirt strengthen the seams. A good shirt will have about twenty per inch.

Fabric: Shirt fabrics, or "shirtings" as they are called by tailors, come in a wide variety of weaves. Cotton is by far the most common material used. Many formal shirts are made of white cotton, which can have a rich, woven texture. A fine white cotton shirt is proper for black tie or white tie affairs. Cotton/polyester blends are also very common. Cotton is breathable, a good conductor of heat, is attractive, and is the standard by which other shirt fabrics are judged. Cotton, however, does wrinkle easily and can be more expensive. Blended shirt fabrics can be wrinkle-resistant, less expensive, and still have a very good look. Too much man-made fiber, however, can make the fabric less breathable and therefore less comfortable on a hot day.

Weaves: Oxford cloth is often used in button-down collared shirts and is suitable for everyday office use. In colored and patterned Oxford shirts, only the threads running in one direction are dyed, while the others are left white. This gives the basket weave fabric its characteristic textured appearance. Pinpoint Oxford is woven of finer yarn making it smoother and more formal. Royal Oxford is finer still. Poplin fabric bears a smoother texture but similar weight, the result of a fine yarn running one way with a thicker one interweaving it. Poplin is soft and comfortable, and often used in more casual shirts. Cotton twill, a diagonal weave, makes for richly textured shirts without sacrificing formality, and is an excellent choice for solid colors. Broadcloth fabric, thanks to its tight weave, displays patterns with exquisite precision.

Collars: At one time, the button-down collar was for sports jackets and casual use, but that rule has mostly faded away, and it is now generally considered acceptable business dress. Whatever collar you wear, it should extend just above the back collar of your jacket.

> **A well-tied tie is the first serious step in life.**
>
> OSCAR WILDE

Sleeves: The cuff of the sleeve should extend a half inch beyond the arm of the jacket when your arm is at rest. This can show off your cufflinks, if the occasion or your personal style calls for them.

Boxers or Briefs?

You might say this is purely a personal question. Mostly that is the case. There are times, however, when one style of underwear fits and looks better than others. Briefs offer more support and are good to use during a workout. Boxers, being looser, can breathe better and might be preferred in hot weather.

How to Fold a Dress Shirt

Costly thy habit as thy purse can buy,
But not express'd in fancy; rich, not gaudy;
For the apparel oft proclaims the man.
—SHAKESPEARE, *HAMLET*, ACT I, SCENE III

If you need to fold a dress shirt to store it in a closet or to pack it, iron the shirt (be sure it's slightly damp first, either from a spray bottle or a cold washing) and let it sit half an hour to cool. Place the shirt frontside down. Grip the left shoulder and hem of the shirt and fold it vertically about to where the collar begins. The sleeve goes horizontally across the back. Now fold the sleeve back over the folded part of the shirt. Repeat these steps on the right side. Now all you need to do is fold the lower part of the shirt up once or twice until it touches the collar. Turn the shirt over and pack or store it.

The Necktie

The purpose of a tie is to add a dash of color, hide the buttons on our shirts, and give a man the sort of squared away look that's impossible with an open collar. Ties are usually made of silk, though woolen neckties are appropriate for winter use and certain sporting outfits (if for instance you go stalking in the Scottish Highlands). In many offices, or at social events, ties can be one of your most distinctive sartorial features, varying from traditional stripes to a wide array of patterns or solids. In some cases, especially in England, the pattern can show your membership of a school, regiment, or club. A regular tie should extend from your collar to your belt buckle. The Windsor knot is a classic for neckties and provides a big bold knot, but the common half Windsor, which is how most people tie their ties, is perfectly acceptable. The bow tie is standard for tuxedos ("black tie") and the most formal evening dress ("white tie") but also favored in business and casual wear by those who like a preppy look.

The Art of the Suit

The cut, color, and fabric of a suit must fit the man, the season, and the occasion. The cut is the most important, which is why custom-tailored suits stand out. They fit. They seem to hang naturally off a man's frame.

Type: The two-piece suit is the most common today. It typically has two buttons and two side vents. The double-breasted suit is more elegant and has become more of a fashion statement for high-priced attorneys, well-dressed professional athletes, and those who want to exhibit a little panache.

The Fit: The proper suit depends on your body type. Today's fashionable skinny suits look best on small-boned, thin men, and are best avoided by very large or portly men, who should also consider wearing suspenders rather than a belt, as they allow pants to hang comfortably and not bunch-up around the waist. Suspenders can also be snappy fashion statements. A man needn't go to London's Savile Row for a custom suit, though that is still the pinnacle. Custom tailors can be found in most cities.

Color: When it comes to business and formal occasions, it's generally best to stick with the traditional colors: dark blue, gray, and black. A brown or light-colored suit is acceptable for weekends or outdoor occasions, but that can also depend on weather and culture. If you're a realtor in LA, lightweight, light-colored suits might be your norm. And in humid climates, seersucker suits are more than acceptable; they can be celebrated as a Southern tradition.

Suit Fabrics

Wool: A pure wool suit is traditional and, depending on the thickness, can fit all seasons. Wool breathes well and will not burn if brushed by a stray cigarette. A lightweight wool, such as "Super 100," makes a fine warm-weather suit. Wool has also successfully been combined with polyester to utilize the benefits of both fabrics, making a moth-proof, breathable, and economical fabric available in a variety of weights.

Polyester: This popular man-made synthetic fabric is lightweight and durable. It can, however, be shiny and does not breath particularly well. In summer these suits can make you feel like you're wearing a raincoat.

Cashmere: A lightweight cashmere suit can be ideal for summer. Cashmere isn't as resistant to wrinkling as merino wool, but it is better than cotton and much less prone to wrinkling than linen.

Tweed: Once synonymous with the fox hunts and proper country weekends, the tweed jacket and suit is now hip again—well, at least in some circles. It's hard to look bad in a well-fit tweed jacket after hours at a hunting lodge, ski chalet, or simply a weekend night out in the country or even the city. It is a fall and winter garment.

Cotton and Linen: Nothing beats a linen suit for a summer evening out. Both of these natural fibers hang beautifully in stony colors. Linen in particular offers options of blends of cotton or even silk. Wrinkling is almost a fashion statement with a linen suit. In the proper place and time this is expected.

The Sports Jacket: The sports jacket today can be an English tweed or a lightweight cotton weave. The patterns, colors, and fabrics used are as broad as those used in the suit. A sports jacket can look great with jeans (something unthinkable a few generations ago) or khakis, or corduroy, or whatever your taste and the occasion warrant. You can't go wrong with a blue sports jacket (or blue blazer), which is the ultimate go-anywhere, do-anything choice.

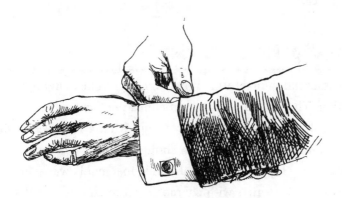

How James Bond's Clothes Changed yet Stayed the Same

James Bond gets his suits from London's Savile Row or, more recently, occasionally from Italy. His look is traditional, but fashionable. Actress Lois Maxwell (Miss Moneypenny) remembered that director Terence Young—*Dr. No* (1962), *From Russia with Love* (1963), and *Thunderball* (1965)—took actor Sean Connery "under his wing" to teach him how to be James Bond. "He took him to dinner, to his tailor, showed him how to walk, how to talk, even how to eat." Young's tailor was Anthony Sinclair, located just off Savile Row on Conduit Street, and his shirtmaker was Turnbull & Asser.

Connery's Bond set the ultimate Bond style, which subsequent Bonds have varied as needed. Roger Moore's English tailors were Cyril Castle and Douglas Hayward. Pierce Brosnan made the Italian Brioni suit quintessential Bond attire. While Daniel Craig has adopted more sporty looks, in every way Bond's taste in clothing—suits, shirts, ties—has always been conservative. Traditional, conservative looks reflect confidence (no need to be showy), authority (a man who knows quality), and respect (putting others at ease with a look that is neither intimidatingly fashionable nor insultingly casual).

Can a Hipster Be a Man?

Style is an individual thing. What is right for one man might not work for another. This has to do with someone's personality, occupation, and his basic role in life. As with everything, what a man wears shouldn't take him out of character—a man should be what he seems. That said, the modern-day hipster is hardly dressing in a manly way. The patterned skinny jeans, the t-shirts with characters from children's TV shows, the fitted hoodies, the courier bags from Freitag, and all that aren't manly—actually, they are boyish on purpose. This doesn't mean hipsters are not good people or something; what a man wears doesn't really tell others whether he is really a gentleman. The hipster clothing, though, wouldn't fit in manly occupations or sports. Can you see someone hunting in such an outfit? Would a Navy SEAL ever dress that way? How about a construction worker? No, the hipster dress is a declaration that someone is not that sort of guy. Again, this doesn't mean a hipster can't be a stand-up man, or even a gentleman, it only means they are purposely not dressing in a manly way.

A Man Carries Things Because He Needs Them

A man carries a briefcase, a gym bag, or a backpack. A man never carries a bag as an accessory. A man carries a bag because it is necessary for what he is doing. His computer bag is to carry a computer so he can work; it isn't around his shoulder because it's from a marque brand and he wants to show off his taste. A man's taste simply is. It is there. It is him. A bag is a part of him because it's part of his life, meaning it has a functional purpose. Women accessorize; men carry things because they need them.

Are Tattoos Manly?

There was a time when tattoos were reserved for sailors, bikers, and enlisted men in the military, and within that realm they were acceptable—and could be statements of loyalty or machismo. Outside of those realms, they were generally frowned upon—or even unthinkable.

Today they are so common as to be symbols of conformity, and machismo has nothing to do with it. In fact, Margot Mifflin, in her book *Bodies of Subversion: A Secret History of Women and Tattoo*, says that in 2012, for the first time in American history, more American women than American men have tattoos. In other words, they've become something on a par with permanent jewelry. The U.S. Food and Drug Administration estimates that forty-five million Americans now have at least one tattoo and confirms that more women than men wear ink in their skin.[2] A big reason for this change has been the evolution of tattoo technology. Advances in applying tattoos have made them safer and far less painful.

Still, despite their popularity, tattoos on a woman can be seen as "slut stamps" and on a man they can be mistaken (or rightly seen) as a symbol of gang membership, and many people, especially those over fifty, can find them off-putting. Tattoos are generally frowned upon by Judaism (see

Leviticus 19:28), and some Christians might consider them graffiti on the temple of the Holy Spirit (your body).

Bottom line: getting a tattoo doesn't make you more manly. If you choose to mark your service in a branch of the military by getting a tattoo, that's one thing, but getting one just because it's the fashion today is something else. Fashions change (which is why tattoo removal services are so popular), but the rules of the gentleman do not.

What About Beards?

Beards are no longer the symbol of a manly man. Hipsters discovered them. They are now worn by a lot of urban men who don't have callouses on their hands. Still, they aren't the mark of a hipster either. Some wear them for fashion, others for practicality. When worn for the latter reason they are more often manly. Lumberjacks, hunting outfitters, and oil men still wear beards because they are out in the cold often where they don't have the opportunity to step in front of a mirror very often. The men who work for Google who wear beards are saying something else entirely.

Don't Dress Like Someone You Are Not

Along with beards, you'll see unlikely urban men wearing plaid shirts, blue jeans, and work boots—pretending to be something they're not—while they sip lattes at Starbucks and type text messages with moisturized thumbs. Tom Puzak at GearJunkie labelled these wannabe men "lumbersexuals." Puzak wrote, "He looks like a man of the woods, but works at The Nerdery, programming for a healthy salary and benefits. His backpack carries a MacBook Air, but looks like it should carry a lumberjack's axe. He is the Lumbersexual."[3]

Some have even been seen sporting fake dirty jeans—like Barracuda Straight Leg Jeans from Nordstrom that retail for more than four hundred dollars and come with fake dirt plastered on them. Mike Rowe, best known as the host of the Discovery Channel's *Dirty Jobs*, ridiculed anyone who might buy the fake dirty jeans. He called such men "inauthentic," and said their pants are "something to foster the illusion of work. The illusion of effort. Or perhaps, for those who actually buy them, the illusion of sanity."[4]

What got us to a place where a store is betting that people will pay $420 (or more) for "dirty" jeans so they can pretend to be something they're not? Talk about someone with a pathetic, inauthentic life. Isn't America supposed to be a place where people roll up their shirtsleeves to get things done, a place where people pull themselves up by their own bootstraps? Are we fast becoming a country of fakers?

America, after all, has long been a place where we ask those we meet, "What do you do?" Europeans rarely ask this question. In Japan this question is actually considered impolite. America, in contrast, was always a nation of doers. It's in our cultural DNA to define ourselves by our hard work. Our value, our sense of self-worth, falls if we don't know how to start a fire, change a tire, or fell a tree—and if you don't know how to do these things, you should learn how to do them, not fake it and try to appear like someone who can (but who can't).

The Right Shoes for the Occasion

In many after-hours or weekend affairs, a man with quality shoes but more affordable jeans, shirt and/or sweater will still fit into good company and will out-dress many other Americans in casual dress.

A standard set of shoes is one pair of brown brogues (full or half), a pair of black Oxfords, and a pair of quality loafers. A pair of good leather boots should be added for any man who will work outside, go to the range, or go hunting.

Brogues: A full or half brogue in brown can be worn with a sports jacket and jeans. It can be worn with some light-colored suits for less formal occasions. A pair of black brogues can be worn with many suits.

Oxfords: A pair of black Oxfords formally worn with closed lacing can be worn with a pinstripe or other formal suit.

> "An otherwise perfect appearance is destroyed, irreparably and at a stroke, if a man has an ugly pair of shoes on his feet. It would be better to go through life barefoot, or wearing just socks, citing religious reasons or the theft of one's luggage, than to lose face by wearing cheap shoes."
>
> BERNHARD ROETZEL, *GENTLEMAN: A TIMELESS FASHION*

CHARLTON HESTON (1923–2008)

I'll give you my gun when you pry it from my cold, dead hands.

—CHARLTON HESTON

Charlton Heston was a man of principle—and though an actor, the image we have of Charlton Heston is the man as he really was. The actor who played heroes, patriots, and individualists was the man who himself marched with Dr. Martin Luther King Jr. to support civil rights for all Americans, regardless of color, and later became president of the National Rifle Association to protect every American's Second Amendment rights to bear arms.

Heston was raised in rural Michigan until he was ten years old. He spent much of his boyhood in the woods, hunting, shooting, practicing self-reliance. When his parents divorced and he moved to the suburbs, he was already a bit of a loner, and lived vividly in his imagination, which led him to acting.

In 1944, Heston married the love of his life, Lydia Marie Clarke, and enlisted in the United States Army Air Forces. He served for two years as a radio operator and aerial gunner aboard a B-25 Mitchell medium bomber, as part of the 77th Bombardment Squadron of the Eleventh Air Force in Alaska. That was not the end of his service. After he gained fame as an actor, he was given the nation's highest security clearance so he could narrate classified military and Department of Energy films (often about nuclear weapons).

During his sixty-year film career, Heston appeared in nearly a hundred movies and was especially memorable in historical spectaculars like *The Ten Commandments* (1956), *The Buccaneer* (1958), *Ben-Hur* (1959), *El Cid* (1961) *55 Days at Peking* (1963), *The Greatest Story Ever Told* (1965), *The Agony and the Ecstasy* (1965), *The War Lord* (1965), and *Khartoum* (1966), as well as in westerns like *The Big Country* (1958), *Major Dundee* (1965), and *Will Penny* (1967), and in classic science fiction like *The Planet of the Apes* (1968), *The Omega Man* (1971), and *Soylent Green* (1973).

He was a tremendous reader, famous for his research into his historical roles, and, as a concerned citizen, extremely well informed on topics of the day.

He was a champion of traditional American rights and was an early and vocal opponent of "political correctness." In an address to students at Harvard Law School in 1999 entitled "Winning the Cultural War," Heston said, "If Americans believed in political correctness, we'd still be King George's boys—subjects bound to the British crown."

He told the students, "You are the best and the brightest. You, here in this fertile cradle of American academia, here in the castle of learning on the Charles River. You are the cream. But I submit that you and your counterparts across the land are the most socially conformed and politically silenced generation since Concord Bridge. And as long as you validate that and abide it, you are, by your grandfathers' standards, cowards."

Heston was what he seemed: a straightforward, talented man of courage and conviction who brought his passion for truth to his art and to his life.

Loafers (or monkstraps): A brown or similar-colored loafer can be worn with casual attire and in some cases with a light-colored suit.

The Belt

The quality of the belt must match your attire. A canvas belt is proper with chinos, corduroys, and such, but never with a suit. A plain black leather belt with a brass buckle is standard for suits worn with black shoes. The basic rule is that your belt should match your shoes.

Cologne

Don't be afraid of cologne. Most men today don't wear it because they've never been taught how, but many manly men of an older generation knew its value. I recently had a stewardess on an airplane lean over to hand me a drink and say, "You smell wonderful. I want my husband to smell like you!" The trick is to make sure your cologne is subtle—a discovery (for women, whose sense of smell is greater than our own) not an announcement (something that hangs around after you leave a room). Make sure the scent suits you—and remember that a little goes a long way.

The Ten Things That Should Be in Your Shaving Kit

After a long plane ride, an overnight stay is so much better if your shaving kit is stocked with these ten quality products.

1. **Soap or Bodywash.** An old-fashioned soap box packed with your favorite soap will make you feel at home when you're away.

> **Advice from the Office Gentleman**
> Dress a little better than you think you should. No one ever lost points for being more polished in posture, dress, and attitude.

> **The Thing about Cuff Links**
> Cufflinks on French cuff shirts are an easy way to add panache to your business attire.

49

2. **A Disposable Razor.** Again, carry what you like to use.

3. **Shaving Cream.** If you wet shave, carry your favorite razor. Otherwise, carry your electric.

4. **Hand Cream.** Even men get dry hands, especially if a trip will have you outdoors or even in the controlled climate of a trade show. Jack Black Industrial Strength Hand Healer is a favorite, but there are many quality brands.

5. **Toothbrush.** You get the theme here. Bring your toothbrush. Don't make do with some annoying travel brush.

6. **Toothpaste.** A smaller tube of your standard makes sense. But also consider a tooth powder for both home and travel. You'll be surprised with how long it gives that dentist-clean feeling.

7. **Deodorant.** Bring your brand.

8. **Cologne.** Bottles are a nuisance when you fly. A solid cologne, like Alfred Lane's Bio or Fulton & Roark's Shackleford, lasts and you don't have to worry about it breaking or spilling.

9. **Lip Balm.** Bring some good ol' ChapStick.

10. **A Multi-Purpose Wipe.** Baby wipes have saved me in backcountry camps. They leave you feeling fresh and clean, not shower clean, but as close as you're going to get without a shower. There are a lot of moisturizing wipes out there; some are even made for men.

RULE 3

BE A
MAN OF ACTION
IN THE WORKPLACE

What you do speaks so loudly that I cannot hear what you say.
—RALPH WALDO EMERSON, *Letters and Social Aims*, 1875

All men feel the pull to be a man of action, a hero. As kids, we imagined acting out that role—maybe as a superhero or a cowboy. It was play, and as we got older this fantasy faded away into us, but it didn't completely go away. We'd all still like to think we'd be a stand-up guy of action if needed. We'd like to think we'd stand up against a workplace monster.

Still, for the vast majority of us being a man of action doesn't mean acting like a character in a Bruce Willis movie. It means being aware and ready to act with professionalism and integrity. In our day-to-day office lives there are plenty of opportunities to do the heroic thing—even if they are simple things.

Almost without exception, whatever your position in the office, you're a leader to someone. If that person needs help with a project—give it. If that person needs help dealing with a difficult colleague—provide it, as a mentor or as a mediator. If that person needs help dealing with a workplace monster—an abusive manager—you can be the one with the cojones to help. And if that person is struggling or failing or is himself a problem—you can be the one to try to set him straight, encouraging him to get his own workaday life in order. All of these actions, in their different ways, take courage. They are also part of your responsibility as a leader.

A leader is aware. He notices when a colleague suddenly becomes disengaged or sullen. He'll sense when something's wrong. It might be something personal, in which case it's none of your business unless he or she chooses to confide in you. But often it has something to do with work. Friendly, subtle inquiries might identify the problem—and maybe, if you're more experienced in the workplace, you can provide the solution. It can be as easy as making sure that person feels a part of the team.

The biggest complaint in many offices is that employees feel there is a lack of communication between management and staff (and sometimes between different departments within a company). They feel they don't know what's going on, that their insights and opinions don't count, and that their efforts are being squandered. That's when a team starts to fall apart. Greg Stube, a Special Forces sergeant, and a true American hero, told me, "When I was on

Green Beret A-Teams, I found it was important not to engender the perception that leaders don't care about those under them. A great way to involve everyone and to foster an environment of full participation and information-sharing is to involve everyone in the planning process. If it isn't practical or possible to have all present during planning sessions, then rapid information dissemination should be made a priority. Don't forget that attitudes go south when people are treated like they don't matter. No communication, no team."

In business, a man of action, a leader, a hero, is a team-builder, because business is a group endeavor. Tapping people's differing talents, encouraging them to take the initiative and take ownership of projects, is heroic leadership, and brings success. "I think this is why free peoples produce greater armies," Stube told me. "We are used to thinking for ourselves." But discipline and hierarchy are important too, he added. "When we also learn to respect orders and our leadership, we become the best we can be. We become thinking parts of the whole. We share our ideas and what we see up and down the chain of command because we are all respected parts of the team. As professionals, we know what to share or to bother the team with and what to keep to ourselves. We know when to keep our mouths shut but also aren't afraid to speak up. That's a hard dichotomy for many to understand—and it might be impossible for someone from an authoritarian state to comprehend. America fosters inquisitive, creative minds; when these men and women also find the discipline to use their creativity and free spirits they can be almost unstoppable. The key to team leadership and execution is fostering and funneling that leadership in the chosen direction according to a plan. This is why often great leadership means getting out of the way."

It is necessary to inspire and protect your people, but what if *you* are the member of the team who is being abused, what if it is *your* boss who is the problem? Many men put their heads down and trudge on, because that's what our fathers and our coaches taught us—and guess what? They were right. That's often the admirable and right thing to do. Stoicism is an effective response to a lot of adversity. If a boss is treating you badly, it might because of other issues happening far above your pay grade—and if something is beyond your control, the rational response is not to try to control it; the manly response is to grit it out.

But, of course, there are times when you need to respond—especially if you think you are being asked to take unethical, or even illegal, actions. It's one thing to quietly endure the normal vicissitudes of business and of a demanding, difficult, or even disrespectful boss, it's quite another to violate your own code of good and decent behavior. If someone asks you do that, you have to say no; and if you can't change the culture where you are, it's time to look for another job.

How to Create the Habits of a Hero

I was sitting in a bar in northern Virginia with a friend of mine, Ben, a member of the Special Forces. A bouncer had asked two belligerent, intoxicated men to leave. They turned on him, looking for a fight, and the bouncer backed up, apparently unsure what to do. It was about to get ugly when Ben stepped in. He grabbed one of the drunks with a wristlock and threw him into the other. Both drunks went down, and Ben was instantly kneeling on one's spine and holding the other's wrist behind his back. Then Ben hoisted them up and walked them out the door.

He came swaggering back, sat down, and sipped his beer. To my look of wide-eyed surprise, he said in a calm, serene tone, "You can do just about anything as long as you do it with confidence, poise, and control."

I was nearly speechless, but he explained: "I was taught that smooth is fast and fast is smooth. I was first taught that as a lesson in gun handling. We'd draw our pistols, bring them up, get the sight picture, and dry fire again and again until the exercise was so tedious our brains got out of the way—a total Zen thing. We wouldn't try to go fast. After a long while you just get fast without any mistakes. That's how you outdraw someone. That's how you kill your target before they kill you."

"But you just took out two guys that even a bouncer was afraid of."

But for a guy who had trained for and seen real combat, this was nothing. "Bar fights are ridiculous. I didn't hurt either of them, not really. They're drunk. Maybe they're good guys. I don't know. Maybe they learned something from being taken down. Doubt it though."

The bouncer stopped by, with a big smile on his face. "Thanks. That happened fast."

Ben nodded. "The smaller one wanted to fight. It was all over his body language."

"But that move you used," said the bouncer. "*Jiu jitsu*?"

"Yeah."

"I gotta learn me some of that."

Ben shook his head. "The trick is to just watch them. Figure out what they're going to do. Run the scenarios through your head. Think about what you need to do. And then do it first, before they even get started."

Ben was done talking about it, but after a while, after the bouncer left, I asked, "What do you mean about fast is smooth and smooth is fast?"

"I've trained to do that physical stuff of course," he said, "but you know, it doesn't take a lot of training in martial arts. It takes staying calm and having poise. You can stay that way because you've already decided what you have to do. Getting there simply takes some forward thinking and preparation. That goes for a lot more than fights. You also have to be prepared for what someone might say, for the tone they'll bring. That's how a man gets himself ready to open a door for a lady or to respond in the right way in a boardroom meeting. You're simply calmer and more ready when you've visualized what can happen and have practiced what you'll do until it becomes natural to you. Most panic, even fear, simply comes from not being mentally prepared."

Want to be hero? Then be calm, be prepared, and be ready to act—and remember that the appropriate response is sometimes to call the police.

I once saw a woman getting slapped around on Main Street in Front Royal, Virginia. I shouted, "Hey!" and took out my phone to call 911. I didn't want to get into a physical confrontation, but as I moved towards them, the woman broke away from her assailant and screamed at me, "Go fuck yourself. You're no shining knight. You come a step closer and I'll kick your ass."

They hopped into his Camaro and gave me the finger as they sped off.

I was dumbfounded, but the fact is stepping into situations like this—where everything seems obvious when it's not and you don't know the nuances of what's going on—can be risky. You could get hurt, of course, but you could also find yourself arrested or sued, however well-intentioned your actions.

So what do you do? I think the best advice comes from former Texas sheriff Jim Wilson: "Take the least amount of physical action possible. You want to help the victim without creating more trouble. Your best bet is to distract the perpetrator until the authorities arrive. Call the proper authorities as soon as you can and let them handle it. Do all you can, if possible, to record everything about the situation. Just don't be one of those people who doesn't help someone in need as you videotape an unfolding tragedy—that is not manly or heroic or even human. Sometimes you *must* act."

But, the bottom line, when you act—do it with caution, do it with premeditation, and be prepared for the unexpected, including ingratitude.

How to Give Credit

Okay, so you might not always get credit for trying to save a woman in distress, but everyone wants credit for their hard work and for their ideas. In the business world if you don't give credit where it is due you will alienate colleagues, destroy their morale, and create dissent that could harm your career. It never lessens your own achievements to share credit or give credit to the team. Give credit sincerely and often, whenever it is justified. Anything less is harmful to the team, shows insecurity, and is unmanly.

How to Be a Handyman Anywhere

How many of us carry a Leatherman on our belts? I've only known one non-tradesman who did. He earned the nickname "Batman" around the office. He liked the nickname and he was always handy. Most men aren't like that. You can, however, still be handy. All it takes are some skills and a humble and open attitude.

1. **Learn the skills.** You should know how to change a tire, use a chainsaw, split wood, sharpen a knife, open a champagne bottle, and more. If you don't then get a copy of *The Ultimate Man's Survival Guide*, this book's older brother.

2. **Use the skills humbly.** It is very manly to teach. This goes for teaching youngsters and women and even other men. Just don't do it arrogantly. Do it simply, well, and humbly.

3. **When you're done don't talk about it.** No one likes a show-off and no one appreciates a braggart. You don't have to worry about people noticing who took charge and solved the problem. They'll know.

How a Man Speaks

Winston Churchill was a man of action. As a soldier, he fought in India, the Sudan, and South Africa, and in the trenches of World War I. He was also a great orator, even though he had to overcome a speech impediment. Most

> **If women don't find you handsome, they should at least find you handy.**
> A RECURRING CATCHPHRASE FROM *THE RED GREEN SHOW* (A CANADIAN TELEVISION COMEDY THAT RAN FROM 1991–2006)

Advice from the Office Gentleman
Online anonymity is helping to protect the weak and to punish the businesses that allow their cultures to become exclusionary or even antagonistic toward women or others. Glassdoor.com is a good example, as it allows employees to anonymously tell others what a workplace's culture is really like.

of us aren't naturally great speakers, but effective public speaking is a learned skill like any other. To communicate your ideas and lead others into action, here are a few tips.

> **Out of the abundance of the heart the mouth speaks.**
>
> JESUS (LUKE 6:45)

- As Shakespeare wrote, "Brevity is the soul of wit." Speak only when you have something to say, and don't use unnecessary words. If you are constantly talking, people will tune you out. Be quick to listen and slow to speak. Delete these crutch words—"um," "like," and "you know"—or any other speech fillers from your conversation. If you need a moment to think of the right word or to connect your thoughts, just pause.

- When speaking to a group, you need to project your voice without shouting. So, when you come to the podium, look out and find the member of the audience farthest from you. Gauge your volume as if you were speaking directly to them, and remember the singer's trick that the strength of your voice should come from your diaphragm rather than your throat. It will give you an authoritative tone without yelling or straining.

- Enunciate and speak clearly. Mumbling can convey a lack of confidence or simply annoy or bore your listener who cannot make out what you say. Listen to a recording of yourself speaking. It can be a humbling experience. It is hard to speak too slowly, but easy to speak too fast. And don't speak in a monotone. Use inflection to keep your voice dancing and people following.

- Practice. Great speakers and great writers have this in common—they practice. Churchill rehearsed his speeches the way an actor rehearses his performance. If you're just starting out as a speaker, part of your practice can be learning from and mimicking the style of other speakers you admire, and learning how they strike the right tone for the right occasion. Your voice should bring fire when heat is needed and be somber and soothing when you need to console someone. Ronald Reagan had a soft voice that offered a Midwestern reassurance of common American decency. Theodore Roosevelt had a high-pitched voice that he used to highlight his high-energy version of "Americanism" and "the strenuous life." John F. Kennedy had a nasally, Massachusetts-accented voice that he packaged as the voice of smart, sophisticated idealism.

- Be expressive and smile. Too many men presume that a manly demeanor is dour, but in fact, that can just be dull. If you are invited, or volunteer, to speak about something, you should be passionate about it, so bring some energy to your speech.

A Posture for Action

The Japanese sword-fighting art *iaido* focuses on the strength a warrior conveys in his posture, movement, and bearing. The word "*iaido*" has been translated as "the way of mental presence and immediate action." *Iaido* is also sometimes called "moving Zen," as it does not emphasize fighting so much as it concentrates on the proper form and controlled body movements that flow into a fight. It is very much the Japanese sword-fighting, martial arts equivalent of "smooth is fast and fast is smooth." An *iaido* instructor, or sensei, will teach his students to focus first on learning how one's deportment, presence, and stature can deter aggression by expressing strength without

> **"I do not believe in a fate that falls on men however they act; but I do believe in a fate that falls on them unless they act."**
>
> G. K. CHESTERTON

59

fighting; only if necessary should a practitioner of *iaido* reach for his sword, and if he does, he does so swiftly with well-practiced movements. Miyamoto Musashi, a seventeenth-century samurai and sword master, wrote of "finding the rhythm in yourself" in *The Book of Five Rings*, a short but profound treatise on the martial arts.

I saw *iaido* in practice when I visited the Noma Dojo in Tokyo.

"This is the way of the warrior," the sensei told me. "But this ancient art has been misunderstood by Americans, and even by many Japanese today. A warrior spirit isn't one who fights. It is one who is ready and able to fight, and by being ready and able, can avoid most fights. A person who masters *iaido* learns to control himself, to be calm and strong and ready to act, but also ready to love with a more open heart."

That is a quintessential Japanese way of looking at manliness, as even samurai warriors would also master Zen arts such as flower arrangement, painting, and the Japanese tea ceremony.

I bring up *iaido* because it emphasizes something our society too often ignores: namely, that strength, posture, self-control, and a presumed capability to fight is fundamental to how men organize themselves in an inevitable hierarchy. Men respect other men who stand up straight, look them in the eyes, have a quiet but assertive voice, and a commanding presence. It really is that primal. As *iaido* teaches, a man will judge another man by how he carries himself. And in difficult situations, the man's man will remember what Sun Tzu wrote in his classic book of military strategy, *The Art of War:* "The supreme art of war is to subdue the enemy without fighting."

It's unlikely that any of us will be called upon to employ the art of fighting with swords, like *iaido*, but from it we can learn the important lesson that a man fights only if attacked, or if it is necessary to protect or save someone else, or if there is no alternative. At such extreme times, former UFC champ Matt Hughes has the right advice: "The person attacking you, or someone else, has already opted not to behave as a gentleman. They are a criminal," says Hughes. "Use any advantage. Fight dirty and be fast and first. Use the bar stool next to you. Go low. Do whatever it takes. And, as quickly as possible, put obstacles between you and disengage. Your only mission is to protect yourself and others and to stop the fight as quickly and humanely as possible. After the fight, all people remember is who won anyway."

Men's Friendships Are Based on Action

Women like to get together to sip chardonnay and talk about relationships. Men don't. They need an activity. They find camaraderie in friendly competition, whether at the bowling alley or at the poker table or in the pool hall or at a gun range. Male friendships are built on mutual experience, which is why most school or office friendships end after you graduate or change jobs, unless they're also grounded in other common interests.

So, a "guys' night out" can be important. But these days, most after-hours social events mean mixed company. So how do you act as a man of action in these circumstances?

The first rule is not to be overbearing. As a man you're naturally competitive, but no one likes an egomaniac, and few people like a showboat. So it's almost always a mistake, for instance, to go into a restaurant, anoint yourself the leader, and order for everyone. The one exception to this rule is if you truly know more about something than your colleagues do, or if you're at a restaurant that you know well, and they don't. If, for instance, you're at a Korean restaurant and you're familiar with Korean food and they're not, it's perfectly acceptable to ask if you can order for everyone (making sure first that you know their likes and dislikes, and any relevant food allergies). It's manly, if you can be an authentic guide to a new experience, because part of being a man is having worldly and practical knowledge. On that score, knowing something about wine and spirits can be useful too.

How to Order Wine

To order for yourself, your lady, or even the table at a business function, follow these gentlemanly rules.

Don't be intimidated into buying expensive wine. Restaurant wines have massive price markups, about double what you would pay at retail. Restaurant owners understand you don't want to appear cheap—and they take advantage of that by putting the highest markup on the second tier of wines. So, don't be afraid to go for the cheapest bottle on the list—at a decent restaurant it'll almost certainly be perfectly drinkable, and you'll most likely be getting better value for your money than if you bought the next lowest priced bottle. The one exception is to avoid "house" wines. These are usually stale wines available only by the glass (they don't want you seeing the bottle). And don't be afraid to experiment with lesser-known labels or regions. Great Cabernet Sauvignons come from Napa, but they also come from Spain, South Africa, and elsewhere, and they're often cheaper.

Glass versus bottle: A restaurant glass is usually about a quarter of a bottle, and is marked up more. So, if you're with a small group, a bottle is usually the better choice, unless your tastes (or meals) are radically different.

The sommelier: It's fine to ask the restaurant's wine expert for suggestions—just be sure that you have a clear idea of what sort of wine you want: a robust red wine to match a steak or a light, dry white wine to go with trout?

Food/wine pairing: The general rule, of course, is red wine for red meat, heavy dishes, and tomato-covered pasta, and white wine for fish or chicken or lighter meals. But the real rule is to have what you want, while being aware that a few very sweet or very spicy foods can overwhelm the taste of your wine. You might need to be careful if you're at an Indian or Thai restaurant, but otherwise, have what you like. And having what you like means it's also perfectly acceptable to have a beer; there's almost as much to learn about being a beer connoisseur as a wine connoisseur. Bottom line, drink what appeals to you—and, of course, never more than you can handle.

Finally, if you do choose wine, and have selected a bottle, the server will begin the wine presentation ritual. First, you will be presented with the bottle to confirm that it is in fact the one you ordered. Don't forget to check the vintage. Servers do accidently pull the wrong wine. The server will then pull the cork and pour a splash of wine into your glass so you may determine whether it's "corked" (gone bad). Give the glass a few swirls to look for grit, then smell and taste. If something is off, tell your server. Any decent restaurant will pull another bottle from the cellar free of charge.

The Art of the After-Dinner Drink

After-dinner drinks can aid your digestion; they can also enrich your social life. Many men relax and bond their friendships in conversations *after* dinner. But what's the best drink for after dinner to keep a conversation flowing?

As with everything, that depends, though the key word is moderation to avoid a hangover. In summer, a light drink, maybe a gin and tonic, rum, or a plum wine, can work, especially if you're sitting out under the stars. If you've been enjoying richer food, or are indulging in a cigar, a whisky or brandy is better. If you want something elegant, a gin martini can be great. Champagne, of course, marks a festive occasion.

Here are a few suggestions for **digestifs:**

Brandy: Brandy is high in alcohol (usually 80 to 120 proof) so it's best to sip in small quantities. It is made from

Advice from the Office Gentleman

We've all heard stories of—or witnessed—people losing it at the office Christmas party. Don't be one of those guys. Have a drink and stop. Or don't have a drink at all. You might be amazed at how entertaining it is to be at such a gathering, keeping your cool and keeping your wits while everyone else is losing theirs. The best advice is be seen, heard, and leave early. You'll see everyone again in the morning—or soon enough.

the wine distillation process. The most famous brandies are Armagnac and Cognac.

Eau de vie: This is a clear, colorless fruit brandy. It's not aged. The main difference from brandy is eau de vie isn't made with grapes, but is made with other fruits. Popular varieties include Schnapps and Calvados.

Grappa: Grappa is made from pomace (the leftover grape pulp and skin from winemaking). Its alcohol content ranges from 70 to 120 proof.

Fortified wine: The reason these spirits are called "fortified wine" is that they are wines that have a spirit added (usually brandy). Popular varieties include vermouth, port, and sherry.

Liqueur: Liqueurs have an added ingredient to flavor them such as sugar, corn syrups, or fruit juice. Liqueurs are usually sweet and are perfect for mixing into cocktails. They are typically lower in alcohol than most spirits (usually around 30 to 60 proof). Popular varieties include: Amari, Grand Marnier, Irish Cream, and crème de menthe.

Hard liquor: If you don't like sweet after-dinner drinks, your best bet is liquor. If you can handle your liquor on the rocks or neat, as a man should, there are few things more pleasurable than sipping a glass of fine whiskey after dinner.

How to Drive Like a Man

This begins by doing the driving. This isn't a fixed rule. You don't lose your man card if your wife or girlfriend drives as you ride shotgun. You do, however, hand her your man card if you don't drive. One of my favorite sights on the road, seen almost exclusively in rural America, is from inside a full-sized pickup truck. The man is driving and the woman beside him isn't way over at the other window. She is leaning against him—using the middle seat belt many full-sized trucks have on their bench seats.

The next rule is to drive as you walk—straight, with confidence, and with the maturity to give way. We all know the (largely true) stereotype of men being unwilling to seek directions. That's because most men want to be independent, in control, and to figure things out for themselves. You can do that—but it can also be time consuming and lead to a lot of detours. Don't be afraid to take directions—either the turn-by-turn directions from a GPS, turning technology to your advantage, or the directions of someone who knows the area better than you do, which might alert you to little known shortcuts or speed traps.

The driver's seat is the power seat. You'll see guys (or gals) get a lot more confident when they drive. Someone driving will suddenly authoritatively say things they wouldn't otherwise. This same person will get much more passive if they are in the passenger seat and might not even talk if they are in a back seat. The girls mostly want their guys to be confident, strong, and assertive—and think that men who aren't those things aren't much worth having. If a guy isn't doing any of the driving, she might lose some respect for him; unless, of course, he has some physical disability that prevents him from driving or if he's an urban sophisticate who walks or takes cabs everywhere.

Why a Man Never Kisses and Tells

A man is a gentleman and a gentleman doesn't kiss and tell. Still, he gives the impression in the way he handles himself that he has plenty of experience in such matters. As he deflects direct questions, he does clearly give the impression that nothing happened. He does not sully her reputation, even implicitly. Discretion is his manner and default position. This is also better

> **Advice from the Office Gentleman**
> Being the designated driver is always manly, because you're the guy who is in control. But if instead of using designated driver, you're getting a cab, be the guy who makes the call, pays the bill, and gets everyone safely home.

GENERAL DOUGLAS MacARTHUR (1880–1964)

Duty, Honor, Country, those three hallowed words reverently dictate what you ought to be, what you can be, what you will be. They are your rallying point to build courage when courage seems to fail, to regain faith when there seems to be little cause for faith, to create hope when hope becomes forlorn.

—DOUGLAS MacARTHUR TO THE CADETS OF THE U.S. MILITARY ACADEMY AT WEST POINT (MAY 1962)

Douglas MacArthur knew all about duty, honor, and country, because he had lived it—and so had his father. His father was a Civil War hero, and later governor of the Philippines. MacArthur's future profession as a soldier was never in doubt. A West Point graduate, he served in the Philippines, in Mexico, and as a brigadier general in the First World War. After the war he was superintendent of West Point and became the youngest major general in the Army.

But what happened to MacArthur in 1932 might have ended the career of a lesser man. He was called upon to disperse the so-called "Bonus Marchers"—forty-three thousand World War I veterans and camp followers (and, MacArthur thought, professional subversives, who had manipulated them) who had marched on Washington to demand payment on bonus service certificates that officially weren't redeemable until 1945. The veterans in the march wanted payment now, because it was the Great Depression, and many had been out of work.

General MacArthur, then-Army chief of staff, was ordered by President Herbert Hoover to disband the marchers, as their protests had turned violent. He did as he was ordered, driving the protestors out by military force. Many thought it was a squalid affair, but MacArthur did his duty, obeying his commander in chief, effectively executing a difficult and controversial job, and dismissing critics as not understanding the reality, and gravity, of the situation.

MacArthur's fame grew massively in the Second World War when he became the supreme Allied commander in the southwest Pacific, and an iconic symbol of America's military commitment and relentless determination to defeat the armies of imperial Japan. The moment he waded ashore at Leyte Gulf, making good on his promise to return to the Philippines, stands with the flag-raising at Iwo Jima as one of the great images of American victory in the Pacific war.

MacArthur accepted Japan's surrender on September 2, 1945, aboard the USS *Missouri* anchored in Tokyo Bay, and he oversaw the occupation of Japan from 1945 to 1951. In 1946 a new Japanese constitution, written by Japanese officials, was brought to him. He looked it over and found it unacceptable. He didn't look to the U.S. Congress or president for his direction. He simply ripped up the document in February 1946 and started over. The new constitution he and his staff created granted universal suffrage to women, stripped Emperor Hirohito of all but symbolic power (but also maintained Japan as a constitutional monarchy, which was important for the stability of the country), stipulated a bill of rights, abolished peerage, and outlawed Japan's right to make war. A massive land redistribution under his watch led to the creation of the middle-class society Japan still enjoys today. No bureaucracy could have managed all that in so short a time.

If this were not enough, MacArthur returned to battle yet again in the Korean War, where his strategic brilliance led to the stunningly successful Inchon landing. Nevertheless, his strategic vision was not shared by President Harry Truman who distrusted MacArthur, worried that he might unnecessarily expand the war, and thought he was insubordinate and usurping the president's role as commander in chief. Truman relieved MacArthur, who returned home to a hero's welcome and an invitation to speak to a joint session of Congress, where he announced his retirement.

When MacArthur said goodbye to the cadets at West Point in May 1962, he said, "In my dreams I hear again the crash of guns, the rattle of musketry, the strange, mournful mutter of the battlefield. But in the evening of my memory always I come back to West Point. Always there echoes and re-echoes: Duty, Honor, Country. Today marks my final roll call with you. But I want you to know that when I cross the river, my last conscious thoughts will be of the Corps, and the Corps, and the Corps. I bid you farewell."

Every gentleman, as a man of action, should aim to live a life of service. He might not live it on the grand stage, like General Douglas MacArthur, but MacArthur's loyalty to the Corps of Cadets can be reflected in our loyalty to our family, our country, and our commitment to working for the benefit others. That is the man of action in the workplace.

for him in the long run, even if he and she really did decide to let something happen, as life will be better in the office for both of them if it doesn't get out.

A Time To Speak: A Conversation with Don Trump Jr.

While promoting my original *Ultimate Man's Survival Guide*, I was asked many times on TV and radio if I could name a real person who embodies all of the traits I argue a man should struggle to attain. I would first say that we are all fallible. No real person is perfect or beyond reproach. I'd then name the people who were ultimate role models for me, starting with the late Floyd Patterson, the former heavyweight champ, as I was lucky to have trained in his gym in New Paltz, New York, and he was everything a man should be to us—honorable, stoic, faithful, courageous, humble, and loving. Floyd showed me and a lot of other young boys the way to becoming all we could be.

For this book though, and especially in this new age, there is no better role model for anyone now in or about to enter the American workplace than Don Trump Jr. I say this after having spent a lot of time around him and around others who know him. I have always found him to be a stand-up man of action. He has outshot me, and so many others, on the range, but never made a big deal about it. He laughs easily and always unabashedly says what he really thinks. He would be celebrated on the covers of *GQ* and *Vanity Fair* and would be treated as the next thing to a Kennedy if he were a Democrat. He is a dedicated father and a conservationist who has a deep love for nature. He carries himself humbly but seriously. He treats everyone with respect. In debates he only tackles his opponents' ideas. He uses the outdoors to teach his sons and daughters the lessons of life. He believes in due process under the law for everyone. He abhors identity politics, as they are in direct contrast to our individual rights and therefore to all that has made America great.

Still, this can be hard for some to see as Don Trump Jr. is, at this moment in the loud history we are living, a political lightning rod. His father is president of the United States, a fact that isn't something the mainstream media and many politicians in the opposing party have been willing to accept.

Nevertheless, he is a living example of all this book espouses. I also say this because, by standing up and honorably fighting for his father and for what's right and true in many speeches, in numerous television and radio appearances, and vociferously on social media, Don Jr. has taken a stand few men would have the courage to take. Also, as he stands tall and pushes back, he isn't losing his cool. Rudyard Kipling said in his great poem "If" that to be a man you must "keep your head" when everyone is "losing theirs," and that is precisely what Don Jr. is accomplishing even as many take his words out of context in attempts to paint him with character flaws he doesn't possess.

Though a gentleman should ideally be composed and stoic in the face of adversity, anyone who has taken the time to read Cicero's *Philippics*—the fiery speeches Cicero gave as he verbally fought Mark Antony for the future of the then Roman Republic—knows that sometimes a statesman or citizen must loudly proclaim what is true even if he is fighting a losing battle. Whole societies can be undone if good men and women don't stand up strongly at the important moments. All the greatest horrors cataloged in our history books could have been prevented if enough strong men and women of character had been willing or able to stand up early on.

To put his stand in context, it's worth remembering that we are a nation founded on the ideal that individual rights are sovereign. Our Bill of Rights is basically a list of restrictions on government that were written and ratified to keep government, or the tyranny of the majority, from usurping our individual rights. One of the most important rights is our freedom of speech. I point this out here because, whether you agree with President Donald J. Trump's tweets or policies or not, you should agree that the First Amendment protection of free speech protects all of us. This is fundamental for many reasons, but one reason is that, as John Stuart Mill once wrote in his great book *On Liberty*, we can't know if something is true and good unless we test the belief against every other idea we or someone else can conjure up.

This is what Don Jr. is doing. He is pushing back against spin, political correctness, half-truths, clever edits of the truth, and complete fabrications by the mainstream media. Just what gives him the courage to do this in an age when a conservative, wealthy, and successful white male is supposed to apologize for existing, is intriguing. I wanted to know how he keeps his manly composure. How does he continually go to college campuses, to political rallies, on television…yet not get rattled or pushed into saying something as vile as what is being said about him or his father.

Don Jr. was kind enough to answer my questions.

What gives you the strength to stand up for what you believe in?

Don Jr.: My father taught me when I was a boy to stand up and fight for what I believe in, but even as I do, to keep a gentlemanly forbearance. That means to fight with honor, with integrity, with compassion, but also not to back down in a just struggle. I never thought I would end up living my life this loudly. I do because I have learned that, when a gentleman has no other choice, he stands up with his shoulders back and faces his adversary in a strong, honorable fashion.

This is such a time. Over the past few years I have spoken out on radio, on cable news, on college campuses, and on social media to push back against and to get around the spin from so many in the mainstream media. During this time I have continuously had my words taken out-of-context and spun. There is no honor in the sophists in the media who play these political games, as they are supposed to be referees calling strikes and balls, but they are instead trying to play the game without ever having stood for election in this great republic; the thing is, as the polls show, the American people see what's really happening here.

Would you advise your sons and daughters, or someone you are mentoring, to stand up in the way you are now?

Don Jr.: Any honorable person should stand up for what is right, but they should do so cautiously and with their eyes wide open. They should not be goaded into losing their temper or behaving in an immoral way. They should treat others with decency and respect, yet shouldn't pull back from doing what is right. If a person in the workplace is being bullied, harassed, or worse, we must speak up even if doing so could cost us a job or even our ability to take care of our family.

That said, there are different ways to stand tall. I would tell someone I was mentoring to listen and learn and be sure they are right before they act. There is a price to pay for being bold. It also isn't always the most effective approach. Before you speak out publicly, you have to make sure you are right and that it is the best way to solve the problem. That said, you can't wait if you witness something extreme, such as a sexual assault. Meanwhile, if you see an attempted public lynching—I am speaking metaphorically here, my media friends—you also can't wait and watch. You must jump into the fray.

As you do so you must keep your wits. You must keep your honor. You must not give up the high moral ground.

Has your stance harmed your business?

Don Jr.: Standing up and loudly fighting for what's right has certainly cost me business. Nevertheless, I can't stay on the sidelines given what is going on. Here we are at a moment when, if you name any economic metric, America is doing better than it has in a long time, yet the mainstream media won't report the facts.

We are in a time when an honorable man like Brett Kavanaugh was subjected to what was clearly a character assassination. This wasn't just done by politicians from the opposing party who don't like his judicial philosophy; it was orchestrated by a huge segment of the media who were willing to say or insinuate anything to destroy the man. At the same time, the mainstream media treated Michael Avenatti, the lawyer who represented "Stormy Daniels," as if he was some savant stepping selflessly into the debate to bring us the light of justice. Ironically, if CNN, the *New York Times,* and more had just looked into Avenatti a little they just might have helped to save Avenatti from himself, as he has since been indicted in California and New York on multiple federal counts of tax evasion, fraud, and embezzlement.

Did you know it would be this vicious of a political fight?

Don Jr.: My father saw all of these one-sided political attacks coming. In June 2015, just after he announced he was running for president, he looked me in the eyes and said, "Now we find out who our friends are."

Though I was a father and I had been a businessman in New York for a long time by then, I was new to politics. I didn't see all that was coming, but my father did. Since 2016; however, I've learned a lot and have become a speaker who is in demand. My social media following is huge. I am in the ring, and have taken some punches, but I'm still coming forward and winning round after round because I tell the truth.

This isn't easy as we're now in an age when the word "man" is treated like a four-letter word by many in the media and in academia. I am also a Republican and the son of a Republican president who is not afraid to tell the American people the truth, so there is a big target on me. Still, in this process, I have found that I don't have a flight gene. I stand up for what's right.

I do this because I watched my father step into the arena when he didn't have to. He had a great life. He had already succeeded by every measure. He didn't need to go into the throes of the political arena. He did that because he knew he could help America become great again. He is doing this at great personal cost.

What in your upbringing do you draw on now for this strength?

Don Jr.: As a boy I spent summers with my mother's relatives in rural Czechoslovakia. At that early age I got to see firsthand what socialism does. I remember my then ninety-three-year-old grandmother crying when we talked about what had happened in her country and as she warned me not to let it happen in America. Now I see a mainstream media pushing us that way and I see indoctrination in that dangerous belief system taking over college campuses. I see this and know it is my responsibility to speak out.

When I was in Czechoslovakia I also was introduced to nature. I learned to shoot and to hunt. Now those things are misunderstood today, but that part of my upbringing taught me discipline and gave me a love for the natural world. It made me into a conservationist. It also helped to give me a base. I grew up on Manhattan's Fifth Avenue. My mother, Ivana Zelníčková, wisely decided that I needed something I wasn't likely to get in New York City. So I was put on a plane for Czechoslovakia, and not for a week or two, but for six to eight weeks each summer. I stayed with my maternal grandfather, a man who was a hunter and fisherman. He taught me how to properly start a campfire and how to hunt and then to eat what we killed. He showed me how to be a country boy.

Those summers might have saved my life. They certainly saved my soul. After those summers, when a lot of our friends were getting into trouble, I was going to bed early so I could be up to hunt turkeys or deer on my father's properties north of New York City. These are lessons I am now teaching my sons and daughters.

That part of my upbringing gave me an appreciation for "flyover America." It also helped to ground me. Now when I get unfairly taken out of context by someone in the media or by someone after I give a speech on a college campus, that hard-earned foundation helps me. I don't get mad. I don't say something out of anger. I simply look at them and tell the truth as a gentleman should. And let me tell you, the truth is a very freeing force.

This honesty doesn't surprise Americans who voted for my father. They expect me to tell it like it is. But it does shock the members of the mainstream media and many in the political class, as they live in a Machiavellian world of spin and half-truths. They honestly don't even know how to deal with someone who doesn't spin, who doesn't play the ends-justify-the-means game. They are baffled by me and my father. They also fear someone who unapologetically tells the truth when the truth is inconvenient to his ends. They then really fear someone who candidly speaks truth right over and around their media filters, as my father does so well.

Are you optimistic about America's future?

Don Jr.: Yes, I am optimistic despite the lies, distortion, and deception I run into every day. I am optimistic because so much of America sees and disapproves of what the mainstream media is trying to do today. I am optimistic because it is in my nature and upbringing to be so. I am optimistic because it's an American trait—we are a people who do the impossible thing of pulling ourselves up by our own bootstraps. I am optimistic because I have watched my father do the impossible.

It used to be that a man was ideally expected to try to be well rounded, to be a Renaissance man grounded on a code who is well read and traveled, who understands and has honed both the physical and the intellectual parts of himself, who is a gentleman, and who will stand up for what's right in small ways around the workplace and in big ways in times of great national peril. I don't want to give up these American ideals. I also don't think most Americans want to give them up.

That's why, in these perilous times in our politics and workplaces, honest guidebooks, like your *Ultimate Man's Survival Guide to the Workplace*, are essential to showing people how to be gentlemen who can survive and thrive today.

RULE 4

BE EXPERT
WITH THE
GENTLEMAN'S
TOOLS

Listen, Bob. A gun is just a tool. No better and no worse than any other tool, a shovel—or an axe or a saddle or a stove or anything. Think of it always that way. A gun is as good—and as bad—as the man who carries it. Remember that.

—SHANE, hero in the novel of the same name[1]

Batman has his belt. Superman doesn't need a thing, aside from his costume. James Bond has his gadgets developed in a secret lab and given to him by Q. A man in the workplace has his tools.

A man's tools, gadgets, and toys are his accoutrements of success. They fill the pages of *GQ, Forbes Life, Car and Driver, Field & Stream,* and *Popular Mechanics*. They can be status symbols—the hip watch, the cufflinks, the smart apps, the sports car—or they can be aesthetic garnishes on his interesting life. They are best when they are useful and honest expressions of who he is.

In the modern American workplace, a man's tools can exhibit thoughtfulness, care, tact, and sophistication. They can save him from calamity and make him the hero of the moment.

The most jarring example I've ever seen of this was when a mouse fell out of a ceiling panel onto the Park Avenue desk of a magazine publisher. There was a scream. People were running. A young man who was an executive assistant was screeching, "Mouse, mouse," in a very high-pitched tone as he hopped on the balls of his feet and as his hands, bent and flopping at the wrists, beat like wings.

An intern from Kentucky calmly walked over to see what the fuss was all about, looked in the publisher's office, and saw a mouse running around on the top of a cluttered desk.

The intern, who is now *Field & Stream*'s hunting editor, pulled out a pocketknife and in one quick motion dispatched the confused rodent. He put the bloody thing in an envelope, sealed it, and dropped it in the trash. The assistant stopped screaming and begged him to please take the bloody thing somewhere, anywhere else, even though it was sealed in an envelope. The intern picked the envelope out of the small trashcan and tossed it in a receptacle out in the lobby. He then went nonchalantly back to his desk and started to work.

He was a rare man in Manhattan still carrying a pocketknife.

Once was a man would have a lighter and a fancy cigarette case so he could offer a smoke to a lady. He would also have a handkerchief to wipe away a tear or a smudge of makeup. Those accoutrements have also mostly faded away with the old-school gentleman.

Still, now we are all Inspector Gadget. The smartphone is the do-it-all gadget that gives us the time, a camera for all events, mapping software to guide us to the restaurant, an app for everything, and even a flashlight if the power goes out—oh, and yes, a phone to call and text with.

Knowing your phone is now a manly thing, though being obsessed with looking at it is hardly manly. A real man shines when the electricity goes out. He must be prepared when cell phones go dead. Such is when his tools and skills are suddenly everything.

Having the right tool at hand, and knowing how to use it, is one of the marks of the gentleman. These days, almost inevitably, one of the gentleman's tools is his cell phone. He's certainly not obsessed with it. But he knows how and when to use it. Here are a few pointers.

The Pocketknife

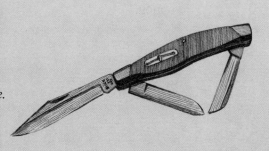

I'll do anything for a woman with a knife.
—JAMES BOND, *LICENCE TO KILL* (1989)

In the city, it's optional—because there are places where it might be forbidden—but if you're stepping off the urban landscape, carry a pocketknife. You'll be surprised how often you'll use it or can offer it to others. The best knives are simple. Don't go for one of those gaudy affairs with big blocky wood handles and a gadget for everything. Pick one that feels comfortable in your pocket and that opens easily. Spyderco has a great collection. It's hard to go wrong with anything from Buck Knives. There are many fine makers of pocketknives.

An Office Gentleman's Smartphone Etiquette

The First Rule of Cell Phones: Except in an emergency, your phone *never* takes precedence over someone who has taken the trouble to come see you. When you have a visitor, switch off your cell phone and put it face down on your desk.

Texts: Never text someone if you can speak with them, and never say anything in a text you wouldn't say in person.

The Screen: Don't walk around the office staring at your phone, and don't sneak peeks at it when you're meeting with someone.

The Call: When you make a call, do it because you have to—not just to while away the time. Remember that your call is disrupting someone's day, so ask them if they have a moment. Be courteous and direct. Never make a call while standing with a group of a people who are engaged in other conversation. And only make a call while driving if your phone has a hands-free option.

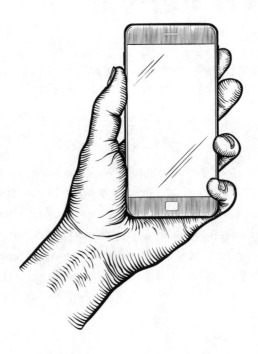

Smartphone Tools

Compass: Most phones have this tool, but most people don't know it's there—or know how to use it. Getting your bearings, knowing which way is north, is crucial to making sense out of the maps on your cell phone and following its directions.

GPS: Of all the benefits of a cell phone, this is probably the most useful. Knowing how to use this tool on your phone can make you the hero if you and your friends others get lost on a hike or in an unfamiliar part of town.

Camera: Even if you're not interested in photography, know how your camera works, because you'll almost inevitably be asked to take someone's photo. So figure out the camera's filters and options and develop some basic photo skills—like how to frame a shot. And sorry, no selfie sticks—they're unmanly.

Thirteen Manly Smartphone Apps

1. **BallisticARC:** This is the app for the rifleman. Plug in your rifle load, and other information, and it will give you precise calculations for the trajectory of your shot.

2. **theScore:** This free app covers the most popular sports, and can deliver team-specific news and scores.

3. **Distiller:** This is a great, free app for whiskey, rum, brandy, tequila, mezcal, gin, vodka, and more, offering a vast array of reviews and recommendations.

4. **Delectable Wine:** This free app allows you to take a photo of a wine label and instantly get ratings and descriptions. It works for many beer and liquor labels as well and is a very useful tool.

Advice from the Office Gentleman

Sunglasses are about function and style. Like other items a man needs they become un- manly when they are no longer necessary. A man who wears dark sunglasses inside doesn't look cool for this reason. Only a rock star or other celebrity can pull off wearing dark sunglasses inside because they're playing a part that is outside manliness—they are something that defies social norms; they are American celebri- ties.

5. **Duolingo:** This app is a smart, fun program to teach yourself new languages.

6. **Sworkit:** Just enter your goals and what kind of work- out you'd like to do and you'll get a personalized work- out plan, with instruction. Sworkit is available for free.

7. **Dark Sky:** This app has to-the-minute local weather forecasts, so you'll know exactly when the rain will start or stop. It costs $3.99, and is well worth it if you're an outdoorsman.

8. **Flightaware:** Airlines aren't always so informative. This free app tracks flights and their status, so you'll always know what's up when you or your friends or family are traveling.

9. **Cocktails Made Easy:** For the cost of a dollar, this app will give you virtually every cocktail recipe ever con- cocted by a bartender.

10. **SAS Survival Guide:** This app shows you how to build a snow shelter, start a fire, dress a wound, and much more. It costs $5.99. It's also available as a book.

11. **UrbanDaddy:** This free app will help you find the right restaurant, bar, or club that has the best of what you want—say, oysters on the half shell—when you want it.

12. **GrillTime:** This ninety-nine-cent app tells you how to grill any cut, thickness, and type of meat to perfection.

13. **Cool Guy:** You can think of this free app as a smart and dapper friend who knows about style and fashion—he might be a little snooty (or hipsterish) at times, but he can also offer good advice.

The Keys to a Man's Wallet

A gentleman's wallet needs to be both functional and presentable. Only a kid pulls out a lump of nylon stuffed with cash, business cards, and every credit card he can get. If you pull out something tattered, overloaded, and spilling cards and receipts, you'll look like an idiot in front of your girlfriend, boss, or client. The only out then is a hell of a good story about why you carry such a pathetic wallet.

The contents of a gentleman's wallet should be pared down to the essentials: an adequate amount of cash, a credit card or two (the average American carries seven), and a driver's license. I also carry my pistol permit and a few business cards. But keep it simple. Photos are better kept on your phone. Your social security card has no business being in your wallet. As for receipts, transfer them from your wallet to a file folder as soon as you get home. To save space in your wallet, use your smartphone to keep photograph copies of important cards and files on a secure cloud-based service or behind an encrypted wall.

There are a few classic wallet styles, including:

- **Leather Billfold Wallets:** Your basic bi-fold or tri-fold wallet in plain black leather is a reliable workhorse. It's perfectly acceptable in just about any social or business setting and holds the daily essentials. It's simple, elegant, and ageless.

- **Sport Wallets:** Usually made from a synthetic weave, these wallets are made in brighter colors and have features which help both secure the items in the wallet and secure the wallet on your person. These are great when you go into the outdoors, but they don't fit in a dinner jacket.

- **Super Slim Wallets:** Often fashionable, these thin but strong wallets force you to carry only what you need— cash, cards, and ID—and don't leave an unsightly or uncomfortable bulge in your interior coat pocket.

- **Money Clips:** Often underrated, metal clips can be eye-catching, and even double as pocket knives. Etsy.com has a great collection.

A Man's Guide to Carrying Guns

James Bond was chastised for his reliance on a handgun with no stopping power in the first Bond movie, *Dr. No* (1962). "M" summons armorer Major Boothroyd to present Bond with a new carry gun. Boothroyd says, "Walther PPK. 7.65mm, with a delivery like a brick through a plate glass window. Takes a Brausch silencer with very little reduction in muzzle velocity. The American CIA swear by them."

Even in 1962 this wasn't true. The Walther PPK in 7.65mm (more commonly referred to as .32 ACP) is such a light caliber that most gun trainers won't even mention it as an option today. John Browning created the .32 ACP (Automatic Colt Pistol) cartridge in 1899 for the FN M1900 semiautomatic pistol. It was popular in the early twentieth century as a carry-gun caliber. It appears often in the film noirs of the Silver Screen age. The .32 ACP didn't hit "like a brick" any more than a .44 magnum could blow a man's "head clean off," as the character Dirty Harry claimed it could. The .32 ACP pushes a 71-grain bullet at about nine hundred feet per second from a four-inch barrel and has about 128 foot-pounds of muzzle energy. Today, even the more powerful and popular .380 ACP (A cartridge that packs just over two hundred foot-pounds of energy, depending on the load, is considered to be too light by most gun experts.)

The standard chambering today for a self-defense gun is 9mm. Some carry larger calibers, such as the .357 Mag., .40 caliber, or the venerable .45 ACP. The downside to these larger calibers isn't just increased recoil; the larger the caliber, or load, the more steel it requires to contain the pressure created when the cartridge is fired. For this reason those who carry concealed are always making compromises between stopping power and gun size, and between comfort to shoot (a full-size gun is much more comfortable to shoot) and comfort to carry (as a smaller handgun is easier to carry). Capacity (many 9mm pistols pack fifteen or more rounds in a magazine) versus power is another compromise someone who wants to carry concealed will have to make.

There is a diverse marketplace in America for those interested in a carry gun. Your first decision will be between a revolver and a semiautomatic pistol. After that you'll have to see what fits you. Many handguns now come with interchangeable grips so you can tailor a gun to your hand size. If you don't know what gun you want, be sure to go to a gun store that offers a wide selection, and preferably offers you a firing range and the option of renting different guns to try them out. And of course if you're a beginner, take a gun training class first. The National Rifle Association has more than 125,000 qualified instructors who can help—and you can find courses near you by going to firearmtraining.nra.org.

Once you've chosen a gun, you can explore various carry options, including popular inside-the-waistband holsters, shoulder holsters, and others. Just remember that over time you'll likely want to carry your gun in different ways, depending on the weather and the occasion.

How to Keep a Ready Mindset for Carrying Concealed

More than eighteen million Americans now have concealed carry licenses (and that's not counting those in the many states that don't require handgun permits). If you take on the heavy responsibility of being an armed citizen, you need to maintain a ready and safe mindset. Here are a few tips from firearms instructors and law-enforcement professionals on how to do that.

1. CREATE GOOD HABITS.

Bill "Doc" Harris, a twenty-one-year Navy veteran who served as a combat medic and is a federal law enforcement instructor, told me that "The difference between a professional and an amateur is the pro does the fundamentals better." To that end, "Training constantly is the key. Don't train at a hundred miles an hour; you should go slow and smooth. You'll speed up as the skills become good habits. This will build your confidence, your familiarity with your firearm, and will instill a healthy comfort level with carrying concealed."

2. THINK LIKE A COP.

Ken Hackathorn, an FBI Certified Firearms Instructor who was in law enforcement for thirty-seven years and who has trained U.S. Military Special Operations forces, says that someone who is carrying concealed should think "like a cop on duty."

Pat McNamara, a firearms instructor and a twenty-two-year veteran of the U.S. Army, agrees: "I tell people to look at it this way: You are your first responder. You are your, and perhaps your spouse's and children's, security detail. You are doing executive protection on a micro level. As you move about society you are not at level 'orange' you are at 'yellow,' just outside the light and ready to be switched on."

Bill Rogers, a former FBI agent and currently chief instructor at the Rogers Shooting School, says, "It's about creating a heightened sense of responsibility and maturity. There are times and places where we know our risk of running into a bad situation is higher. You need to turn up your radar in these places."

Doc Harris adds, "You shouldn't live in fear. You are carrying so you can defend yourself and others in a crisis. It's like being a parent with a young child. You are always scanning ahead of them and around them for potential trouble—for traffic in a parking lot, a loose dog or whatever. It's the same when you're carrying concealed. You need to stay aware."

Julie Golob, a world-class shooting champion, made an important point when she said, "It's easy for some to confuse preparedness with paranoia when it comes to personal defense, but the differences are significant. A paranoid person lives in constant worry and fear, whereas someone who has prepared appropriately is aware, confident, and capable. One who chooses to take responsibility for their own safety doesn't leave things to chance….It's one of the most powerful choices you can make for yourself."

3. NEVER BECOME TOO COMFORTABLE.

The experts agree that complacency can be a problem. Ken Hackathorn warned that "You'd better stay aware of your gun. The environment is always changing."

Il Ling New, an instructor at Gunsite Academy, underlined for me the importance of staying aware in a world full of distractions. "Don't let texting, phone calls, or even window shopping shift your focus from what is in your immediate area. Our visual processing decreases when we listen to someone speak, as a result, cell-phone users make great targets. And need I say anything about those who virtually eliminate one of their most important defensive sensors by filling their ears with ear buds?" She added bluntly, "Don't look like food. Eye contact alone can help eliminate you from a criminal's wish list. Our intuition is amazingly accurate. Listen to and trust your gut."

Pat McNamara summarized his advice by saying, "Don't become cocky."

Advice from the Office Gentleman

Everyone has a smartphone now, so who needs a watch? Anyone who wants to show style does. A fine watch is one of the distinguishing features of a refined man, offering its user both fashion and utility. And a fine watch doesn't have to be a traditional model; it can be a modern sports watch, because many of these are handsome and useful. A watch is not mere jewelry but a tool that can serve a variety of functions.

The Manly Pen
Always have a good pen on you—not only for your own use, but because few things make a greater impression than loaning someone a fine pen.

Ken Hackathorn underlined that, noting: "Going from white to red all in an instant is a hard transition. At that point you are going to fall back on training because you won't be able to think clearly. The decades I spent in law enforcement taught me that. You are much more likely to make good, smart decisions if you are trained properly and mentally aware and humble so that you give yourself a moment to react in the best way possible."

A Businessman's Office and Desk

A carry gun is a tool for an emergency. Your desk and your office, on the other hand, are essential to the successful conduct of your day-to-day business activities. They should be as neat, well-organized, and well-turned-out as your personal appearance. In a business setting, they're essentially one and the same. A messy desk will make you look disorganized and like a slob, just as much as if you had papers falling out of your pockets and tomato stains on your tie. For the most part, it's best to go minimal on office décor, but a few well-chosen books, pictures, and knickknacks can be conversation starters—the outward symbols of an interesting life. We can't always choose our office furniture, but we can choose to keep it clean and tidy, and to highlight a few things that inspire us, motivate us, and remind us who we are and what's important.

The Card Deck

A man should know how to handle cards. He should be able to distinguish between and rank (in this order) the basic hands in poker: royal flush, straight flush, four of a kind, full house, flush, straight, three of a kind, two pair, pair, and high card. And besides poker, he should be able to play at least a few games like blackjack, gin rummy, solitaire, and maybe bridge. Cards are one of the great icebreakers in social life, and one of the best and most inexpensive means to entertain yourself or a group of friends.

A Gentleman's Car

For most of us a car is another essential tool—and one where, again, personal preference and usefulness are combined. For me, I drive a pickup truck, because it best suits my lifestyle. It might not suit yours. And a man can express himself with his car. You might like the feel of a sports car. Or you might prefer the power of an American muscle car. Or you might choose the reliability and affordability of one of today's bestselling sedans. Or you might indulge an automotive hobby: restoring a classic in your garage that you take out only on sunny Sunday afternoons. The only absolute rule is that you take care of your car as you take care of every other fine tool that you own—keep it clean and functioning at a high level.

A Man's Guide to the Mixed Drink

A man's bar is a storehouse of tools. He needs to know how to use them to make a mixed drink. Some are simple—gin and tonic, rum and coke, whiskey and soda are all self-explanatory. Others take a little more know-how. Here are some classics:

> " Alcohol is like love," he said. "The first kiss is magic, the second is intimate, the third is routine. After that you take the girl's clothes off. "
>
> RAYMOND CHANDLER, *THE LONG GOODBYE*

1.   **Martini:** Fill a beaker with crushed ice. Add two and a half ounces of dry gin (preferably Beefeater) and half an ounce of dry vermouth (preferably Dolin or Noilly Prat) and stir until there is a sheath of frost outside the beaker.

Strain into a five-ounce cocktail glass and garnish with a sliver of lemon peel.

2. **Boilermaker:** Fill two-thirds of a pint glass with beer and then drop a shot of whiskey into it. That's an old-school, working man's mixed drink.

3. **Tom Collins:** There's a special Tom Collins glass you can use, and there are variety of ways to mix it up, but all you really need is a normal, cold glass filled with ice. Add two ounces of gin, a dash of sugar or an ounce of sugar syrup, three quarters of an ounce of lemon juice, and soda water (to taste) garnished with a cherry or lemon peel. It's great for a hot summer evening.

4. **Manhattan:** This is a Prohibition-era drink that combines two ounces of rye whiskey, half an ounce of vermouth, and a dash of bitters, with a maraschino cherry garnish.

5. **Old Fashioned:** Take two ounces of bourbon or rye whiskey and pour into a glass loaded with a sugar cube, a splash of water, and a dash or two of bitters. You can garnish it with a maraschino cherry or an orange slice.

6. **Godfather:** This drink is as simple and straightforward as a man should be, mixing an ounce and a half of whiskey or bourbon with three quarters of an ounce of Amaretto.

PHILIP MARLOWE

It was about eleven o'clock in the morning, mid-October, with the sun not shining and a look of hard wet rain in the clearness of the foothills. I was wearing my powder-blue suit, with dark blue shirt, tie, and display handkerchief, black brogues, black wool socks with dark little clocks on them. I was neat, clean, shaved, and sober, and I didn't care who knew it. I was everything the well-dressed private detective ought to be. I was calling on four million dollars.

—RAYMOND CHANDLER, *THE BIG SLEEP*

Philip Marlowe is a fictional private detective created by the author Raymond Chandler in a series of manly novels set in the environs of mid-twentieth century Los Angeles. Arguably the best of the novels are *The Big Sleep*, *Farewell, My Lovely,* and *The Long Goodbye*. Humphrey Bogart was the classic movie Marlowe in the film adaptation of *The Big Sleep* (1946).

Marlowe is a bachelor who lives by a rigid, incorruptible, self-sacrificing gentleman's code, like a modern knight, though he keeps his ideals and idealism hidden behind a tough, cynical, hard-boiled exterior. He is a man of some culture—a reader and a chess player—though he makes no show of it. He is courageous and can handle himself in a fight. He liked whiskey or brandy and consumed both in quantities that would impress a Hemingway character. In *The High Window*, he gets out a bottle of Four Roses. At other times he drinks Old Forester, a Kentucky bourbon. In *The Little Sister*, he says (the novels are in first person), "I hung up and fed myself a slug of Old Forester to brace my nerves for the interview. As I was inhaling it I heard her steps tripping along the corridor." In *The Long Goodbye* he and Terry Lennox drink gimlets.

He dresses well, out of self-respect and respect for others, but he is not a dandy and his office is spartan.

Marlowe doesn't work for the government, as a police officer or a secret agent. He is a resolute individualist, a maverick, a man who can walk away from temptation, and, while created by a British-American writer (Raymond Chandler) is a quintessential American hero.

Philip Marlowe is a gentleman who knows how to use the gentleman's tools—including a gun and a cocktail shaker—but who knows that the gentleman's greatest tool, what makes him most useful to others and to himself, is having a stainless steel character.

> **Advice from the Office Gentleman**
>
> Discretion might still the better part of valor, but now it's our devices that are tattling on us. Apps and more record where we go and how long we stay there. This data can be easily taken out of context—but it can also be made available to law enforcement and is increasingly used as evidence in divorce cases. The moral is: know and use but never trust the technology you carry with you.

7. **Stinger:** This is a drink James Bond, Cary Grant, and Frank Sinatra drank—and if you have one too many you'll learn exactly how it gets its name. It's two ounces of brandy with three quarters of an ounce of white crème de menthe liqueur.

8. **Rob Roy:** Named after Robert Roy McGregor, "the Scottish Robin Hood," it combines an ounce and a half of Scotch whisky, three quarters of an ounce of sweet vermouth, and a dash of bitters.

Utilizing the Tools of a Spy

We are all spies now—and we're all spied upon. We now live in a society where we have to assume everything we do outside of our homes is being recorded by a security camera or by someone's phone. It's important to know to use this technology to your advantage—and avoid others using it to your disadvantage.

For instance, if you're in a car accident—after you've called the first responders and taken any other necessary action—you might find it useful to record where the vehicles are, the extent of the damage, and statements from witnesses so that the facts don't get misrepresented later.

Similarly, if you are in a meeting where what is discussed might later be disputed, you might want to record the conversation—though be sure you do so lawfully as many states require that you inform the other parties and have their consent before making recording. But don't count on the law to protect you—you need to protect yourself and you should also always assume you're being recorded, and that your comments might be leaked.

I remember one time when I did a live debate broadcast over the Internet. With about ten minutes to kill before the official airtime, the host and my opponent in the debate chatted with me, and it was obvious they were trying to get me to say unguarded things. I knew better. I saw the camera was on, and I knew that if I wasn't careful and precise in everything I said, they'd take something out of context and turn it into a YouTube hit piece. They finally gave up and we started the debate. When I left the studio, I found out that they were actually streaming live from the minute I walked into the room.

RULE 5

TREAT EVERY
WOMAN AS A LADY

I don't think there will be a woman prime minister in my lifetime.
—MARGARET THATCHER, on the BBC in 1973

I think male prime ministers one day will come back into fashion.
—MARGARET THATCHER on TV-AM in 1988 after having been prime
minister of the United Kingdom for almost a decade

O ffice romances are notoriously tricky—even when both parties do their best to keep things professional, quiet, and low-key. I knew one apparently star-crossed couple—I'll call them Mark and Mary—who tried to do everything right, but one of them got the other fired.

She was new in the office, just out of grad school. All the guys noticed her. If they didn't, they should have. She wasn't a Marilyn Monroe broadcasting a look-at-me sex appeal with flirtatious glances and a walk that made men stop. She was appropriate in the office on New York's Park Avenue. She just couldn't help her looks and how they made men feel in the Manhattan office.

He was two years older, and in a different department. They took pains to avoid gossip, even leaving separately and meeting at out-of-the-way restaurants for lunch where they wouldn't be seen.

But he still got fired.

I was there the morning they let him go. He had packed up his belongings in a box, and looked bewildered. I followed him outside and we went to a coffee shop. He started to tell me about Mary.

The day before, she had passed him in the hallway. They did not acknowledge each other. In fact, Mark was talking to a colleague, but the colleague turned and nodded at Mary's departing figure and whispered, "You hittin' that?" Mark didn't know how to respond, so he just smiled and walked away. But a woman in a nearby cubicle overhead the crass colleague, and passed the news to Mary.

Mary fretted all afternoon and finally left the office early feeling sick. She met Mark that evening and confronted him. She was scared her career would be derailed by gossip and that she would be made out as the office harlot. Someone told her that he had another office romance in his past, and that woman had left. Did this sort of gossip drive her away? Mark tried to reassure her. He said that yes, he had gone out with another woman in the office, but that had nothing to do with her departure—she had been offered a better position downtown—and that it hadn't been much of a relationship anyway, though they were still friends. Mary didn't find that comforting—in fact, she worried about his motives. She reminded him that she had not encouraged his advances—and in fact had deterred them initially. But he had been boy-ishly persistent and she had finally consented to go out with him as long as he kept it quiet. Now she worried that he was using her—regarding her as an affair, something he could brag about, to score points with men at the office. It made her feel defiled—and his denials didn't help. She thought it was damn-ing that he hadn't confronted his crass colleague, hadn't told him to grow up, hadn't defended her honor.

That morning she went to human resources. She later said she didn't want Mark fired; she just wanted to know her options. But the company moved immediately to protect itself from any potential lawsuit for sexual harassment by dismissing Mark.

"Look, I know there are monsters out there," Mark said, glancing at the glass high-rises outside the coffee shop. "But I'm not one of them. I'm still nuts about her. Well, I don't know how I feel now. She did this to me. All I did was fall for her and she got me terminated. Maybe I should just forget about her. Maybe she's poison."

They laugh about it now.

They are married and live in a Midwestern city and have two kids and good careers, though for different companies.

"This wasn't some #MeToo thing," she says. "I guess I just didn't know what would happen. I didn't understand how things are. How could I? How can anyone? Things are changing so fast. And they need to, I mean, there are some very bad guys out there. But there needs to be common sense, too. We need rules, a process that's fair that protects the vulnerable and that doesn't just punish men by default."

In the end, Mark handled the situation relatively well. He kept his head. He was polite to the head of human resources. And obviously the story had a happy ending. But it also highlights how fraught the office environment has become between men and women.

The modern gentleman knows there's a big difference between chivalry and sexism. Mark's crass colleague was sexist in making a crude remark. Chivalry, on the other hand, is about treating women with deference and respect. Chivalry is also about self-control, upholding what's right, and defending other people, including women. If Mark had defended Mary by telling his colleague to grow up, he might have saved himself a lot of trouble, and put office gossips in their place.

There is nothing wrong—and everything right—with holding a door open for a woman, or letting her onto the elevator first, or offering her your coat on a cold night or your umbrella when it's raining, or extending any of the other simple courtesies that men used to routinely extend to women, and that made the interactions between men and women a little more pleasant and cordial and kind. I only once had a woman get mad at me for opening a door for her. It was in Manhattan, and she was young and pretty and getting too much attention from guys on the staff. She said, "I can open doors for myself." I smiled and said, "I'll remember that." Months later she apologized. By then she'd become engaged to one of the men in the office, she no longer felt threatened by all the male attention, and she realized that not all of us were wolves.

Men obviously have to do a better job—and have to realize that many women still do feel threatened or harassed or in danger around men. Some women interviewed for this book confessed that they can be nervous or fearful walking alone in some urban areas after dark. These days, a man often can't offer to walk a woman to her car after a business dinner without arousing comment, but you can be the leader who ensures after a late business dinner that a group of you gets everyone safely to their cars.

We also need to accept that "no" means "no"—and that is true everywhere, especially in the office. Littler things are important too. We might think it's flattering to compliment an office colleague on her looks. Don't—even if you think your comments are completely harmless and well-intentioned. I was in a meeting once when an older gentleman from Kentucky looked across the Manhattan conference room and called attention to a new graphic designer, saying, "And I want to say it's good to have Kimberly on staff. She is by far the prettiest girl in the whole department." The poor girl blushed and the rest of us bit our tongues. The gentleman from Kentucky, a very nice fellow, was quickly ushered to a closed-door meeting and told to never, ever comment on anyone's looks again. He "meant well," and was baffled that his comments were deemed offensive. He came from a more innocent time, when admiration was not deemed harassment. But these days, you need to avoid complimenting people on their looks; and you also need to be very careful about it after hours, socializing, say, with colleagues at a bar. Work follows us everywhere, and so must our self-awareness. Self-control is one extremely important measure of a man—and it's as important now as it ever was, governing not just your actions but your speech.

Lieutenant General Robert Baden-Powell, who created the Boy Scouts, came up with the rule that a scout is clean in thought, word, and deed. However old-fashioned it sounds, there's no better advice for a man in the modern office. And you can update it by adding: "The man in the office is clean in thought, word, and deed—and well aware that his intentions might still be misconstrued, and so must be even more careful."

Don't Talk Down to the Cute Secretary

Don't call the smoking hot secretary "a hottie" or even "sweetie." When talking to colleagues avoid old-fashioned labels like honey, baby, darling, young lady, or young man. These remarks can be seen as putdowns. Instead, use their names. Also, never use gender-based insults such as bitch or slut. If you must insult someone, call attention to the fault in their actions—they are a "slob in the office kitchen" or "someone who shouldn't have a second drink at an office holiday party."

Don't be Afraid to Call a Lady "Ma'am"

Former Senator Barbara Boxer of California made headlines when she chastised a general during a Senate hearing for calling her "ma'am." She said, "Do me a favor, can you call me senator instead of 'ma'am,' you know, it's just a thing, I've worked so hard for that title."[1] This became such a thing that *Saturday Night Live* did a skit on it. Though it is military dogma to use "sir" and "ma'am," this general was polite and did as she requested. That is how a man acts. If a woman specifically asks you not to call her "ma'am" or even a "lady," simply respect her opinion whenever possible. This also goes for anyone who is questioning their sexual identity or identifying as something their physiology indicates they are not. Don't smirk. Be polite.

How to Do an Office Romance

Office romances are not necessarily forbidden, and don't always have to be kept secret. We all know people who have met their spouses this way. And office relationships are common. CareerBuilder.com did a survey of three thousand people from many fields and found that 38 percent had dated someone from work.[2] But such romances have to be done carefully, thoughtfully, maturely, and with discretion, because careers can be derailed when office relationships go bad. You still have to see that person every day. One woman interviewed for this book said when her office relationship ended she felt that she was "in an episode of *Survivor*," as their sales team divided into competing

How to Use a Unisex Bathroom

I recently stopped by Vassar College's wonderful library, and had to use a restroom. Every one I found was "gender-neutral"—and they weren't private one-stall things by an open floor plan unisex mixer. I went in one and saw that all the stalls were thankfully empty. When I was washing my hands, two girls, presumably students, came in, stopped, and one said with disdain, "Oh, there is a guy in here." I said, "Now wait a second. That's labeling. How do you know how I identify?" She rolled her eyes, said, "Whatever," and left in a huff. Maybe, just maybe, experiences like this will convince this generation that "men's" and "women's" designations make sense with bathrooms after all.

camps. He eventually moved on after she'd defeated him in the war for alliances. And it is true that in this #MeToo era, men are, as a rule, it seems, more likely to end up the losers, and more likely to be terminated.

So how do you pull off a work relationship without getting fired?

1. Check your employee handbook and know your company's policy on dating coworkers. Many companies only bar relationships when the employees are in the same department and one reports to the other. These policies are designed to prevent favoritism and block the use of pay and promotions for ulterior motives.

   Sometimes companies require employees to inform the human resources department if they have a relationship with a coworker. This has a weird "Big Brother is watching over you" vibe, but a few of the people I interviewed for this book said that they thought it was necessary. In some cases, they were actually transferred to other departments to prevent any appearance of a conflict of interest, and they appreciated that human resources did this to protect their careers.

Advice from the Office Gentleman
If you ask a co-worker on a date and she says "no," don't ask again. If she reconsiders, she can ask.

Other companies have taken more drastic measures. Some have flat-out banned relationships between employees—good luck with that—and a few companies have gone off their rockers. NBC actually ordered its employees to rat out colleagues who are having office romances. If an NBC employee doesn't tattle on a co-worker, he could be fired.[3] This policy was part of a sexual-harassment overhaul NBC undertook after they fired *Today* show host Matt Lauer when sexual-harassment claims against him went public.

"Romantic relationships at work are not exactly unusual, but now NBC says it is taking a zero-tolerance approach," someone told PageSix.com. "Staffers have been told that if they find out about any affairs, romances, inappropriate relationships, or behavior in the office, they have to report it to human resources, their superior, or the company anti-harassment phone line."[4]

2. Should you keep the relationship secret from coworkers? This depends. At first, certainly. But if the relationship becomes serious, it is time to let it out. Keep it professional, but people are going to find out and it will be better if you, rather than office gossips, control the narrative.

3. Think before you act. CareerBuilder.com found that 7 percent of those who had office romances left their jobs after the romance ended.[5] As a gentleman you need to take your relationships and your career seriously. So don't take on an office romance lightly.

4. Don't post anything about your relationship online. Colleagues at work will routinely link to your social media, because you're friends—and obviously they'll notice.

5. Don't flirt over the company email. You may think your work email is private, but courts have ruled otherwise. Your employer does have the right to read your emails.

Does the "Mike Pence Rule" Make Sense?

Many in the mainstream media have mocked, or even vilified, Mike Pence for abiding by the rule of never having dinner alone with a woman other than his wife. But in the #MeToo era is that really such a bad rule?

Sheryl Sandberg, the CEO of Facebook, thinks it is. "In the aftermath of #MeToo, as several powerful men have lost their jobs (good!) for harassing women, some men have chosen to react by adopting what's called the Mike Pence rule—never having dinner alone with a woman other than your wife," she wrote. "If men think that the way to address workplace sexual harassment is to avoid one-on-one time with female colleagues—including meetings, coffee breaks, and all the interactions that help us work together effectively—it will be a huge setback for women."[6]

Needless to say, that can be true, but nevertheless, men in today's workplace should be very cautious of being alone with a woman in the office or in social settings, especially when alcohol is present. A misconstrued word or gesture could lead to an accusation of sexual harassment. An older male friend of mine was even chided by human resources for telling a female employee in a closed-door performance review that he was going to have to "take her to the woodshed" for some of her failings on the job. For him it was just an expression; human resources warned him that it could be taken as a physical threat.

Sandberg wrote: "Long before the #MeToo movement, a lack of mentorship from senior leaders was already a significant barrier for women in the workplace. New numbers indicate that this is getting worse: a recent survey by Lean In and SurveyMonkey revealed that almost half of male managers in the United States are now uncomfortable participating in basic activities with women. Senior men are 3.5 times more likely to hesitate to have a work dinner alone with a junior woman than with a junior man—and 5 times more likely to hesitate to travel for work alone with a woman....The last thing women need right now is even more isolation. Men vastly outnumber women as managers and senior leaders, so when they avoid, ice out, or exclude women, we pay the price. Men who want to be on the right side of this issue shouldn't avoid women. They should mentor them."[7]

Sandberg is clearly right that men are reacting to the #MeToo environment by becoming very careful. This certainly can reduce opportunities women have to network and build stronger work relationships with their bosses and colleagues. Nevertheless, in a climate where men are considered guilty before perhaps being proved innocent, this Pence rule is rational, as one misunderstanding can end a career.

"As for the Pence rule—if you insist on following it, adopt a revised version," says Sandberg. "Don't want to have dinner alone with a female colleague? Fine. But make access equal: no dinners alone with anyone. Breakfast or lunches for all. Or group dinners only, nothing one-on-one. Whatever you choose, treat women and men equally."[8]

Anyone who has ever traveled for business knows it's rarely that simple. It is often necessary for business teams to be broken up at trade shows, sales calls, off-site meetings, and so on.

Sandberg also avoids addressing a truth so old it is in the Old Testament. In Proverbs we read the warning that "the lips of the adulterous woman drip honey; and her speech is smoother than oil; but in the end she is bitter as gall, sharp as a double-edged sword" (Proverbs 5:3–4). If a man does mentor a woman and at some point she pursues him to have an affair, what happens if he rebukes her advances? Will she turn on him out of anger or embarrassment, and accuse him of harassment, of leading her on? If he is innocent and denies her accusations, what are the chances that he'll be believed in the #MeToo era? What business, to avoid liability, wouldn't fire him first and ask questions later? (Interestingly, many women interviewed for this book said women are much harder on other women than men are—many men feel protective and lenient towards younger women—and given that men are often the ones making the call, they're more likely to fire another man. This unconscious or instinctive bias might be mitigated by bringing more women into helping make these decisions.)

In a corporate setting, in-house attorneys are often brought in to manage away any serious situation; sometimes by settling with the accuser and getting her to sign a nondisclosure agreement. The risk of having to pay such cash settlements is another factor driving male managers away from mentoring female employees. But it also cuts the other way: sometimes nondisclosure agreements protect people who are guilty of vile conduct.

That seems to be what happened in Congress, in how it dealt with sexual harassment claims against members. Congress put the burden of proof on accusers and in some cases—we don't know how many—used procedural means to keep them silent. Congress even used a slush fund to quietly pay some accusers.

In the corporate world, forced arbitration agreements are used to keep claims out of court—and so out of the public eye. But some companies, Microsoft for example, have found them to be a public relations liability; they have ditched forced arbitration agreements from their employee contracts and have actually called on Congress to make them illegal.[9]

So, in the light of all this financial and legal risk, the Mike Pence rule seems a sensible precaution in the workplace of today. The best way to avoid trouble, after all, is to avoid situations where there could be any doubt.

How to Defend Women (and Men) in This Age of the Hashtag

Joseph Campbell, a famed professor of myth, once said that the trick for a married couple to keep a long and lasting relationship is for them to successfully shift from "passion to compassion." It seems that our culture needs to do the same. The #MeToo movement is a passionate movement—and it's done a lot of good in exposing bad guys. But we need to move on to the next step and establish a better working relationship between the sexes.

We begin by exerting self-control. Though stoicism is often misunderstood by the mainstream today, a gentleman learns to be stoic so he can control himself when we need him most, such as in a crisis or when a truly bad dude is in the office; a gentleman toughens himself by tackling real things in life; a gentleman, by definition, endeavors to be a well-rounded man who helps and defends women.

At the same time any reasonable man realizes that equal rights between the sexes are an ideal in law and practice that has yet to be fully realized in the workplace or society, and that maybe it will never be completely attained, as men and women are different and all of us are fallible. Still, the ideal is lofty and good nonetheless.

Actually, the basic truth that all people have the same rights in their political, economic, and social lives is thousands of years overdue. The fact that we are all equal before God, and therefore in rights, is a basic Judea-Christian principle that once challenged the "divine right" of kings and empowered English juries to judge as they saw fit. The idea that every person is equal in rights to every other person spread over the Atlantic and gave the world the wildly successful American experiment. This basic and beautiful concept flowered in America and has, over the past two centuries grown at least in principle to include everyone, no matter their race or gender, and that's a beautiful thing.

Surely the popularity of Jordan Peterson with young men is a step in the right direction. Consider this passage from his massive bestseller *12 Rules for Life: An Antidote to Chaos*: "Aim high. Set your sights on the betterment of Being. Align yourself, in your soul, with Truth and the Highest Good. There is habitable order to establish and beauty to bring into existence. There is evil to overcome, suffering to ameliorate, and yourself to better."[10] This is another call to chivalry. And the more we can get back to the ideals of the gentleman,

FRANK SINATRA (1915–1998)

The big lesson in life, baby, is never be scared of anyone or anything.

—FRANK SINATRA

The late Michael Thomas Kelly, a writer and editor for the *Washington Post*, the *New Yorker*, and the *Atlantic*, blamed the king of cool, Frank Sinatra himself, for messing up American ideals about manliness. He notes that Sinatra was perhaps America's first true pop idol of the Entertainment Age. Kelly wrote that "what Frank Sinatra projected was: cool." Before cool, there "was smart (as in the smart set)….The pre-Frank hip guy, the model of aesthetic and moral superiority to which men aspired, is the American male of the 1930s and 1940s. He is Humphrey Bogart in *The Big Sleep* or *Casablanca*."[11]

The old-school American gentleman might have been more like Rhett Butler in *Gone with the Wind*. He might appear suavely cynical, but deep down he adhered to the old values of patriotism, honor, and courage, which was why Butler joined the Southern war effort, even as the South was crumbling.

But Sinatra's cool was different: "Cool was looking out for number one always. Cool didn't get mad; it got even." Cool, as Kelly pointed out, is a cad.[12] Cool isn't pious and certainly isn't virtuous. Cool is looking out for himself. Cool can be cynical about women. As Sinatra famously said, the trick to understanding women is "You treat a lady like a dame, and a dame like a lady." And cool can relish having links with mobsters and the Mafia as something dangerous and exciting.

But there was more to Sinatra than that. He was a man of famously long friendships, especially with his "Rat Pack" buddies. He was loyal.

He was hardworking. He was intent on being a good father to his children. He could be compassionate and generous. He stood for racial equality when it took guts to do so and became a Republican in Hollywood, supporting Richard Nixon and Ronald Reagan when that took guts too. For many men of the greatest generation, he might not have been the moral equal of Philip Marlowe, but there was toughness to admire in the skinny kid from New Jersey who became not just a teen heartthrob, but a mature, thoughtful actor and singer who wouldn't back down from anyone and insisted on doing things his way.

Sinatra played himself perfectly in the movie *The Tender Trap* (1955), as a debonair man-about-town, a sophisticated and wealthy bachelor in New York City who has mobs of attractive women chasing him. But at the end of the film, Debbie Reynolds wins him and pulls him back into convention, and he becomes a good husband.

Sinatra might have been cool. He might have bucked some conventions, but he upheld others. He was definitely a big-city version of man's man. But his life and the movie *The Tender Trap* highlight something else: that sometimes a woman of character is required to bring out the true gentleman beneath the man-about-town. To modify Sinatra's line, maybe the trick to getting along in the office is for every man to treat every woman as a lady, and for every woman to demand that every man be a gentleman.

the better off our society will be for men and women. As one woman on Wall Street told me, "I'm tired of dating weak metro men. They're boys—forever weak and juvenile and so afraid to offend. They make me nervous, because when they do break the bounds, like children they don't know how to control themselves—they seem to have none of a gentleman's strength. I want a man—a strong gentleman."

A gentleman's strength comes from his character—and when it comes to improving our national character, men and women both have a role to play. I graduated from a military college with women as fellow cadets. I've run with the bulls in Pamplona alongside men and women. I've hunted dangerous game with men and women. I've gone spelunking into caverns and climbed cliffs with men and women. Along the way I've found that some of the most courageous and honorable people doing these things with me were women. I've also met and interviewed many fine police officers, U.S. Marines, and firefighters and know that some of the best among them are women. Strong character is something that can unite us, whatever our chromosomes. The goal of each and every one of us should be to be stand-up, strong, compassionate, courageous, and honorable individuals.

RULE 6

DEVELOP A GENTLEMAN'S PHILOSOPHY

"What is the worst of all evils, Socrates?" asked Cebes.

"That the soul of every man is compelled, through experiencing some extreme pleasure or pain, to imagine that whatever most strongly arouses such feelings is most vivid and real—although, of course, it is not; and these things are chiefly the things that can be seen....This, then Cebes, is why the true lovers of learning are moderate and manly...."

—PLATO, the dialogue of Phaedo

man isn't the sum of his genetics, nor is he a pawn of his culture and environment, though those are influences on everything about him. A man is the sum of his decisions. His decisions, if he is a thinking man, as a gentleman must be, are propelled by his passions and controlled by his code. His code or creed is a summation of his hard-earned philosophy, the gentlemanly rules he struggles to live by.

A man's decision to understand himself—just look around and you'll see this is hardly a given—is the most important and recurrent decision he'll make.

A man's decision to respect himself comes as a consequence of endeavoring to understand himself. His decision to respect others logically follows—hence the Golden Rule.

A man's respect for women starts with his mother—even, or maybe especially, if she is or was not all she should have been. He knows that all women are potential mothers, and that motherhood is a life of self-sacrifice, service, and necessity if the human race is to prosper. As Mark Twain said, "Where would men be without women? Scarce, sir, mighty scarce."

A man's decision to have empathy and not to give up that empathy by degrees with the pain of life is fundamental to his ability to become and to remain a moral man. The gentleman is imbued with the spirit of chivalry, of strength put at the service of others.

A man's resolution to be a hero—or a villain or something in between—will shape his life's story. Will he confront life bravely as a hero, will he cut corners chasing some vision of self-interest, or will he placidly follow where others lead? Each is a choice, and each takes a man down a different life path.

How open-minded a man decides to be is a decision, as he must internally confront political correctness, cultural bias, and so much more that will shape him if he fails to think for himself.

If a man decides to think for himself, as best he can, then he will learn along the way that for his decisions to be made well it helps for them to be earned in sweat and blood—with skin in the game. The gentleman knows that what Theodore Roosevelt called the "strenuous life"—challenging one's self, competing in the arena—matures a man. It brings earned wisdom. He finds that too easy a life won't mature him and that too horrible a life might wreck him and could even turn him into something he should abhor.

A man should then come to understand that human history teaches plainly, even bluntly and with horrifying repetition, that we are all capable of becoming horrible things if we don't have the courage to think and act for good despite the peer pressure, the temptations, the horror, or even the dictates of an immoral institution, boss, or government.

Decision by decision a man grows, provided he is a thinking man, not another sad case of arrested development. Along the way he learns he can't control anything, not really, except how he takes it. This understanding leads to another level of decisions. He realizes why stoicism is a fundamental part of manliness, because it is the exertion of self-control. He finds how a man can keep his head in a crisis and thereby save a life or protect someone in need. And he knows that the gentleman, ultimately, is the stand-up man of action, a man who strives always to improve himself so that he can help others.

The Dozen Rules That Build a Gentleman's Philosophy

1. EVERYONE IS EQUAL AND MUST BE JUDGED SOLELY BY THEIR WORDS AND ACTIONS.

Every individual has a spark of divinity in them. They are all equal in rights and before God. This is a basic Judeo-Christian principle and central to the American experiment in freedom, but today it is not well understood, and it is certainly not promoted in academia or popular culture or the mainstream media. It is nevertheless how the gentleman regards others, especially in the workplace.

A gentleman knows that appearances, while important, can be deceiving, which is why the gentleman looks beyond them to see a person's character. That's not always easy, of course. We are all strongly influenced by first impressions, by a person's physical appearance, dress, mannerisms, and body language—and it is fine to register all these things. But the gentleman knows there is more to a person, there is character. And character is what could make the handsome, finely dressed man a villain or a slovenly hotdog vendor a hero. It takes self-control, maturity, experience, and training for a man to see past appearances, perhaps especially with women.

Seeing past appearances is even harder today because of the perversities of "identity politics," which demand, in the name of "equality" that we judge everyone by race, ethnicity, sex, and too many other categories to list, in order, they say, to redress historical inequities. But their goals are not really about justice or even true "diversity." Their goals are about power and manipulating people, because they assign labels to groups and expect people within these groups to think within narrow ideological confines. A gentleman not only doesn't fall into this trap; he stands apart from it. He supports true diversity—freedom of thought—and judges people solely on the content of their character.

2. A MAN WORKS. HE CREATES. HE DOESN'T LIVE OFF OTHERS AS A PARASITE.

To a certain degree a man is what he does. Work is where a man exercises his knowledge and skills. Work is in large part how a man contributes to society, to serving others. Work is one way that a man fills his life with purpose; it is how he earns a living for himself and his family. It is an arena in which he displays his core competencies. It is where he shows himself, in practical terms, worthy of respect (including self-respect). Any man who lacks work will also lack a sense of self-worth.

A man's work, of course, goes beyond what he does at the office. His life's work might be, in part, a building he erected or a deal he secured, but it is much more than that. Ultimately, it is to have lived his life well—and for many men, that means a successful marriage and well-raised children and providing for them through hard work.

3. A MAN THINKS FOR HIMSELF.

Not thinking for yourself means you are someone else's tool. Ernest Hemingway said, "The most essential gift for a good writer is a built-in, shockproof, shit detector. This is the writer's radar and all great writers have had it."[1] That's true not just for writers but for all real men. It's too easy to be led by the crowd and to adopt other people's opinions as your own. Seek counsel, read, and learn—and then come to conclusions based on your own experience and the experience of others (including the lessons of history).

4. WHAT DOES NOT KILL A MAN DOES MAKE HIM STRONGER.

Nietzsche was generally right when he said this, and it is a good way to look at adversity: as something to be overcome, as an experience from which we can learn and profit. Grit, strength, and fortitude are manly. Giving up isn't.

5. THERE ARE REAL RULES TO THE GAME AND WE ARE KEEPING SCORE.

Everything is not relative; our natural rights are not subjective. All cultures and subcultures are not equal. Some lead to freedom and prosperity; others lead to barbarism. If we study history, we can keep score about what brings success to a civilization and what doesn't. And what is true at the level of nations is true at the level of the individual. There are rules that guide human conduct. Some lead to better outcomes than others. Some lead to trust. Some lead to suspicion. Know which is which, and guide your own conduct accordingly. And keep score, it will help you to recognize the office liar, thief, and backstabber.

6. A MAN IS SOMEONE WHO CAN DEFEND OTHERS—AND HIMSELF.

The gentleman is never a bully and never goes looking for a fight; if a fight can be honorably avoided, he avoids it. But he is also a hero at heart. He will not allow himself or others to be bullied or abused; and he will never back down from a just fight.

7. A MAN KNOWS HOW TO DO THINGS.

Any man who can't change a flat tire has just given up his man card. A man is a doer. When he doesn't know how to do something, he finds someone who does and learns. Part of being a doer is being a lifelong learner and knowing that when one is confronted with a problem, he takes a deep breath, keeps his cool, stays calm, and devises a rational solution.

8. A MAN'S CREED DOESN'T CHANGE OR EVOLVE, IT IS FOUND.

The Ten Commandments represent eternal, universal truths. The gentleman's code is similar. It is a discovering of what is true and good in manly behavior. Joseph Cardinal Ratzinger, Pope Benedict XVI, cast this wisdom in theological terms: "Meaning that is self-made is in the last analysis no meaning. Meaning, that is, the ground on which our existence as a totality can stand and live, cannot be made but only received."[2] A gentleman doesn't make things up; he seeks, discovers, and embodies the truths of manhood.

9. A MAN IS SHAPED BY EXPERIENCE.

Everything a man does adds to his stock of knowledge, his skills, his character, his ability to triumph over adversity—from the scraped knees of a boy on his bike, to the middle-aged man trying to teach himself a new language, to the elderly man reflecting on a life's reading of the classics. Every effort we make, every challenge we overcome, every task we undertake will determine the sort of man we are, increasing our understanding, building our strength, and adding to our sense of empathy. Gandhi said, "The weak can never forgive. Forgiveness is the attribute of the strong."[3] Properly lived experience gives us that strength.

10. A GENTLEMAN MUST BE WHAT HE SEEMS.

The politician who lies, the mechanic who makes unnecessary repairs, the reporter who pretends to be your friend before attacking you in print—none of them are gentlemen. A gentleman cannot be a hypocrite; he sets himself a high standard and he has to live by it. That doesn't mean he will always succeed, but he will be measured by the sincerity with which he makes the attempt.

11. A MAN DOES WHAT NEEDS TO BE DONE—NOT JUST WHAT'S POLITICALLY EXPEDIENT.

Some of the manliest stands in history occurred because someone stubbornly stood up for goodness in the midst of corruption, for what is morally right against injustice—and did so regardless of the consequences. Jesus did this and changed the world for the better. Saints did this too. In smaller ways, whistleblowers do this and so does anyone in an office who stands up for the weak and the abused.

12. A MAN TRIES TO UNDERSTAND AND SHAPE THE WORLD AROUND HIM FOR THE BETTER.

The gentleman is a practical man. He accepts reality, seeks to understand it, and lives in the world as it is. But that doesn't mean that in his conduct and his actions he is not an influence for the betterment of his society. There are few things more powerful than a good example. The gentleman, by endeavoring to live a good and noble life of kindness and service, courage, and courtesy, of work and endeavor, is one of the best examples any society can have.

> "There are only two or three human stories, and they go on repeating themselves as fiercely as if they had never happened before."
>
> WILLA CATHER, *O PIONEERS!*

The Modern Office Gentleman Is on a Hero's Journey

Joseph Campbell (1904–1987) studied myths and religious stories across time and civilizations and found there are striking similarities in the narrative structures of heroic tales. He explored this discovery in his famous book *The Hero with a Thousand Faces*. The book had a major impact on the storytelling of major filmmakers like George Miller, Steven Spielberg, George Lucas, and Francis Ford Coppola. Knowing its basic framework can also help any man assess the trajectory of his life and career.

When we enter a new workplace, we step into a new challenge, a new competition, and we will have to surmount new obstacles. Our everyday business life can seem like a slog, but if we think about it correctly, it can be a hero's journey. That, too, is part of the gentleman's philosophy.

Here are the twelve stages of the hero's journey:

1. **The Ordinary World:** This is our starting point, where our journey begins—and the back-story that brought us here. It is our normal life: growing up, going to school, perhaps the early steps in a career.

2. **The Call to Adventure:** There is a disruption to the ordinary world—a challenge, an opportunity, or maybe a threat—and the hero, who initially might be reluctant to act, to leave what he knows, is called into an adventure.

3. **Refusal of the Call:** The hero's initial reluctance gains ground—he fears the unknown and would rather avoid the dangers inherent in the adventure.

4. **Meeting the Mentor:** The hero comes across a sage who restores the hero's courage, and gives him training, equipment, or advice that will help him on the journey.

5. **Crossing the Threshold:** The hero commits to leaving his ordinary world and entering a dangerous new place with unfamiliar rules and values.

6. **Tests, Allies, and Enemies:** The hero is tested by challenges, sorts out allegiances, and discovers who might be an enemy and who might be trustworthy.

7. **Approach to the Inmost Cave:** The hero and new-found allies prepare for the major challenge of their journey.

8. **The Ordeal:** The hero faces a setback, the possibility of failure, defeat, or even death. He must overcome his fears, recover from the setback, and march on.

9. **The Reward:** The hero, having overcome his ordeal, wins a prize or seizes a treasure—and while he might celebrate this accomplishment, he recognizes that he could also lose it.

10. **The Road Back:** The hero is driven to complete the adventure, to return to the ordinary world, his mission accomplished.

11. **The Resurrection:** The hero is severely tested once more on the threshold of home, and is purified by making a final sacrifice and overcoming his most dangerous challenge.

12. **Return with the Elixir:** The hero returns home. He looks back on his journey with new knowledge of himself and the world; and while this journey is over, another might begin.[4]

This is the plot outline of many legends and enduring stories, because it speaks to the human desire to make sense of our experiences, to see our

> **[The] women [who supported Judge Brett Kavanaugh] are gender traitors, to borrow a term from the dystopian TV series 'The Handmaid's Tale.' They've made standing by the patriarchy a full-time job. The women who support them show up at the Capitol wearing 'Women for Kavanaugh' T-shirts, but also probably tell their daughters to put on less revealing clothes when they go out.**
>
> ALEXIS GRENELL, *NEW YORK TIMES*[5]

lives as a story. Cast yourself in the role of the hero on the journey and you might find that it helps illuminate your path.

How to Ethically Navigate the Mainstream Media's Political Use of #MeToo

A year after the #MeToo movement began, the *New York Times* reported that, by its count, "at least 200 prominent men had lost their jobs after public allegations of sexual harassment."[6] As is usual with the *New York Times* (or the *Washington Post*), this news feature reads like an opinion piece—booing the bad guys who have been toppled and cheering on the good gals who have often replaced them. (The story's headline is, "#MeToo Brought Down 201 Powerful Men. Nearly Half of Their Replacements Are Women.") For the mainstream media and academia, the importance of #MeToo is less about the merits, demerits, or justice of individual cases than it is about pushing a political narrative, a narrative that can have a dangerous influence on your workplace. The office gentleman, to protect his career and to defend what's right, needs to understand the politics behind #MeToo and know why the leftist agitators who promote it are wrong, and the *Times* article offers a handy summary of most of the claims of the movement.

1. THEY TREAT ALMOST ALL MEN AS IF THEY'RE BAD GUYS.

Joan Williams, a professor who studies "gender" at the University of California, Hastings College of the Law, told the *New York Times*, "We've never seen something like this before. Women have always been seen as risky [to hire], because they might do something like have a baby. But men are now being seen as more risky hires."[7]

In the mainstream media—or in academia—that sort of assertion is accepted with nods of approval, but it is, obviously, absurd. It implies that the number of men who commit sexual harassment or assault is statistically comparable to the number of women who choose to have children. According to a Pew study, 86 percent of American women choose to have children. Is Williams saying that business leaders now assume that more than eight out of ten men are, or will be, guilty of committing sexual harassment in the workplace? Or is she, like most media commentators, merely stating her prejudices, in this case that all men are likely to abuse women?

The problem is that ridiculous allegations like this are often promoted by academia and the media and accepted by the fearful or the credulous, or because it fits a narrative that people want to believe. The gentleman needs to be wary. Don't assume common sense in your workplace managers or even among your colleagues.

2. THEY WANT MORE GOVERNMENT POWER.

The *Times* story alleges that "Sexual harassment has hardly been erased in the workplace. Federal law still does not fully protect huge groups of women, including those who work freelance or at companies with fewer than 15 employees."[8]

The article argues that the federal government should assume more control over private contractors, through more laws and regulations against sexism or sexual harassment. That might be a good solution for a government bureaucrat who wants to meddle with the private sector but is certainly a bad solution for business and workers because of the law of unintended consequences. When I was employed by Time Inc., the Clinton administration tried, via a lawsuit from the Labor Department, to force magazines to treat freelancers as fulltime employees with benefits. If you're a government bureaucrat, you might think that this lawsuit would help workers. But, had this lawsuit succeeded, it might have given some freelancers benefits, but it would have cost many more freelancers their assignments as they were priced out of the market.

Additional government regulations and bureaucracy will certainly increase the harassment of businesses and contractors, but it will do nothing to stem sexual harassment. According to circumstances, sexual harassment is already a crime; and in a competitive job market, small-business owners who get a reputation for harassing employees aren't likely to stay in business long. This is just another case of advocates of big government taking a "crisis" to push for even bigger, more intrusive government that in the end only subverts small businesses, limits opportunity, costs jobs, and in the process lessens our freedom.

3. THEY LITERALLY SAY WOMEN ARE BETTER THAN MEN.

According to the *Times* article, "Women's personal experiences, including as mothers, can make workplaces more welcoming to other women." Moreover, "Research has repeatedly shown that women tend to lead differently. In general, they create more respectful work environments, where harassment is less likely to flourish and where women feel more comfortable reporting it. Female leaders tend to hire and promote more women;[9] pay them more equally; and make companies more profitable.[10] Women bring their life experiences and perspectives to decision-making, and that can help in business because women make the vast majority of purchasing decisions. In government, women have been shown to be more collaborative and bipartisan, and promote more policies supporting women, children, and social welfare."[11]

Can anyone believe this? Well, again, don't be too sure that common sense will prevail. But if everything the *Times* and its cited studies say is true, it begs the question of why businesses bother to employ men at all. The people interviewed for this book told me what any commonsensical person would already know: bad managers can be male or female, and so can good managers. Some women I interviewed even said that female managers were often harder to work for—perhaps overcompensating, wanting to be as tough as men are supposed to be, and not wanting to be seen as biased toward women.

In your own conduct, follow the gentleman's rule of treating everyone equally, but realize that not everyone in your office will agree with your philosophy or follow your example.

4. THEY SAY THE SYSTEM IS STILL PREJUDICED AGAINST WOMEN.

The *Times* article states that "The women who have risen…can only make so much change—they are still operating in a male-dominated system."[12]

While it is true that in 2017 women only held 26 (or 5.2 percent of) CEO positions at S&P 500 companies,[13] it is also true that in 2017 women held more than half (51.5 percent) of management, professional, and related positions in all American companies.[14] That is especially impressive given that many women leave the work force, at least temporarily, when they become mothers. In 2015, the labor force participation rate for parents with children under the age of eighteen was 69.9 percent for mothers and 92.7 percent for fathers.[15] And the percentage of women who choose to stay at home to care for their children rises the younger the children are. (In 2017, 61.5 percent of women with children under three were in the labor force.)[16]

In addition, some industries, such as in healthcare and primary education, have been largely taken over by women—78 percent of healthcare and social assistance workers are now women, while 77 percent of hospital employees are women.[17] Other job categories, such as those in science, technology, engineering, and math, remain largely male, because, however unpopular it is to say it, men, tend to be more interested in *things* (and how they work) or statistics, while women tend to be more interested in *people*, a truth to which anyone who has actually socialized with men and women can attest. Given the freedom to choose their own professions, men and women won't necessarily choose the same things, though this can vary greatly with any individual man or woman.

The gentleman doesn't blame "the system"—America's free market economy—for his failures. A man is not a victim. He considers himself the master of his own fate, and he doesn't see justice as demanding across-the-board equal results. (In fact, he would regard this as evidence of likely injustice, because it was probably achieved by force.) But he needs to recognize that some people *do* define themselves as victims. Some people find such self-pity "empowering"—and wherever identity politics succeeds, it can be empowering to those why cry victim the loudest.

5. THEY SAY THE PUNISHMENT FOR SEXUAL HARASS-MENT OF ANY KIND MUST BE A LIFE SENTENCE.

"More than 10 percent of the ousted men [punished for alleged sexual harassment] have tried to make a comeback, or voiced a desire to, and many never lost financial power," according to the *Times* article, which added, "When people accused of harassment return to power without making amends—or never lose it, at least financially—it limits the post-Weinstein movement's potential to change how power is exercised in American society."[18]

The gentleman believes that redemption is possible. That is, after all, another fundamental Judeo-Christian principle. This is particularly important when someone is ousted from a job for alleged sexual harassment and didn't get a public trial. If the accusations were a matter of rumor, or innuendo, or misunderstanding, or misguided (but not criminal) behavior, the gentleman believes that justice is served if the ousted employee is given the opportunity to learn from the experience and gets a second chance.

If the accused is guilty of rape or assault, that is obviously a criminal matter, and a different issue. But if the "crime" was something as harmless, if stupid or juvenile, as telling a dirty joke or sharing a racy photo, a lifelong punishment with no chance at redemption is just vindictive.

> There is only one corner of the universe you can be certain of improving, and that's your own self.
>
> ALDOUS HUXLEY

How a Man in the Workplace Must Reconcile Honor with Duty

Loyalty to an employer, or a friend, or an institution, is a gentlemanly trait. And a gentleman's first reaction when an employer, friend, or institution goes wrong is to stand by them and quietly guide them back to where they should be. But every gentleman ultimately recognizes a higher loyalty, a higher duty, that goes back to first principles, which can be tested in extreme circumstances.

Consider Dietrich Bonhoeffer (1906–1945). Bonhoeffer was a Lutheran pastor, theologian, and author who became an anti-Nazi dissident in Hitler's Germany. In June 1939, he accepted an invitation from the Union Theological Seminary in New York, which would allow him to stay in the United States, safe from Nazi persecution, but he soon regretted his decision. He wrote to Reinhold Niebuhr, an American theologian, "I have come to the conclusion that I made a mistake in coming to America. I must live through this difficult period in our national history with the people of Germany. I will have no right to participate in the reconstruction of Christian life in Germany after the war if I do not share the trials of this time with my people."[19]

Bonhoeffer returned to Germany, knowing that his opposition to Nazi policies, and his support for the anti-Nazi resistance movement, could cost him his life. The Gestapo arrested him in April 1943, and he was eventually sent to a concentration camp. In his absence, he was tried, found guilty of conspiring against Hitler, and sentenced to death.

His judge was Otto Thorbeck. Thorbeck, like many Germans, had to decide where his duty lay. He believed that his duty was to the Nazi regime. He pursued that duty so fervently that even as Nazi Germany was collapsing, he insisted on witnessing that the death sentence was carried out against Bonhoeffer. When his train broke down, he rode the rest of the way to the concentration camp on a bicycle. He saw that Bonhoeffer was taken out of his cell, stripped naked, and hanged at dawn on April 9, 1945. Two weeks later the United States 90th and 97th Infantry Divisions liberated the camp where Bonhoeffer had last been held.

Eberhard Bethge, a student and friend of Bonhoeffer's, quoted a man who saw the execution as saying, "I saw Pastor Bonhoeffer...kneeling on the floor praying fervently to God. I was most deeply moved by the way this lovable man prayed, so devout and so certain that God heard his prayer. At the place of execution, he again said a short prayer and then climbed the few steps to the gallows, brave and composed."[20]

Thorbeck is now a footnote in history, but Bonhoeffer is a man who has inspired millions. Bonhoeffer was loyal to his country, his people, and most especially his faith—and he knew he had a higher loyalty than to the Nazi regime.

Even in the day-to-day circumstances of our humdrum business lives there may be times when we have a higher duty than merely following the dictates of our bosses. There are times when even we might need to take a stand.

Make Sure Your Business Has a Clear Code and Stands by It

If you're in a management position—and this decision is not above your pay grade—make sure your company has a code of conduct that reflects the company's daily operations, core values, and culture. Many companies rely on committee-drafted codes of conduct that are a combination of legal "cover your ass" and self-congratulatory corporate marketing mush.

One of the worst company codes of conduct I've seen is Google's. At one point it says, "Google is committed to advancing privacy and freedom of expression for our users around the world. Where user privacy and freedom of expression face government challenges, we seek to implement internationally recognized standards that respect those rights as we develop products, do business in diverse markets, and respond to government requests to access user information or remove user content."[21]

Anyone familiar with Google's business with the Chinese government must blanch when reading that statement, though lawyered phrases like "seek to implement" give Google plenty of room to maneuver.

Better codes of conduct can be found at the Coca-Cola Company, which, in forty-four pages, tells employees exactly what is expected of them.[22] The Hershey Company has a good thirty-page explanation of what it stands for.[23] And IBM has an excellent thirty-one-page declaration outlining goals and expectations.[24] All of these are worth reading, but the best summary of a worthy corporate creed comes from Magpul Industries.

Richard Fitzpatrick, the company's founder and president, had a series of principles that he wanted his company to follow. These eventually became what he calls "The Magpul Foundations."

While some of the "foundations" represent provocative business principles—such as "Build what they need, not what they want,"—others represent the broader philosophy behind the company. In a section titled "Annoy the Establishment," the company affirms that Magpul "stands on the side of the individual. The natural enemy of the individual and innovation is the establishment and bureaucracy (which literally means 'the power of the desk'). When we are annoying the establishment, we know we are effectively upholding our principles." The entire Magpul Foundations statement is reproduced in Appendix III.

The Gentleman Knows That Work Is about Physical Reality

Outside the realms of theory, where academics live, or opinions, where most journalism exists, or ideology, where politics thrives, there is real life—and real life is a tangible, physical thing. It is where we do business, and it is where men learn to prove themselves.

I once had the opportunity to meet a dozen students at the South African Wildlife College who were taking a course to become professional hunters. They were learning to track game, survive in the bush, deal with poachers, and other necessary skills.

As part of their training, these college-age students had to stalk to within twenty yards of dangerous game—rhino, elephant, lion, hippo, and Cape buffalo—in Kruger National Park. And then they had to slip away safely, knowing that a shift in the wind, or a failure to move silently or camouflage their movements, could bring an elephant or lion charging to kill them. The students had to master their fear as well as their bush skills, and they needed to know how to shoot in order to defend themselves and others in their party.

As part of their training, they had to sit blindfolded for hours alongside a river frequented by crocodiles and hippos or by a watering hole used by lions, hyenas, elephants, and other wild game. A retired game ranger was nearby with a rifle, in case things got too dangerous—though the students weren't told this. The goal of the exercise for was not merely for the students to conquer their fears, but to heighten their senses of hearing and smell.

One twenty-year-old student told me, "It's deathly frightening, but you feel so alive. You start to smell things you didn't know you could. You hear things and sort them out….The primal fear sharpens you. There is nothing more terrifying than being certain you hear a leopard or a lion close and coming. But still you have to keep control. Running would only trigger a predatory response. You have to master the fear to pass this part of the course."

Every job has its own dangers. Every employee is subject to certain fears. The gentleman is the man who masters fear, who stays calm in times of danger, and who knows that what he does in this world is not solely a matter of ideas or opinions but of hard physical fact; it is a matter of real-world success or failure, even do or die. That's another way that the gentleman's philosophy is grounded in reality.

WILL ROGERS (1879–1935)

I love the man that can smile in trouble, that can gather strength from distress, and grow brave by reflection. 'Tis the business of little minds to shrink; but he whose heart is firm, and whose conscience approves his conduct, will pursue his principles unto death.

—THOMAS PAINE, *THE AMERICAN CRISIS*

There used to be a time when to be an American was to be a man of grit, optimism, and common sense. Few men embodied that ideal better than Will Rogers. He was a common man, a cowboy, part Native American, who represented the good-humored, practical, and modestly idealistic American way of thinking. He was the common man's philosopher, and a true American gentleman—gaining that status not by birth but by the content of his character.

Will Rogers famously said that he never met a man he didn't like—or, to give the full quote: "I joked about every prominent man in my lifetime, but I never met one I didn't like." He punctured pomposity, ridiculed extremism, and was the antithesis of the grandstanding ideologue. He once said, "There is nothing as easy as denouncing….It don't take much to see that something is wrong but it does take some eyesight to see what will put it right again."

Rogers came from a relatively prominent family in Oklahoma, but he dropped out of school to make his way in the world. He became a working cowhand, and later an entertainer who gained success on stage, in the movies, on the radio, on the lecture circuit, and as a newspaper columnist. He used his fame for a variety of good causes, including encouraging the development of the aviation industry in the United States. He was an easy-going, reasonable man, with a gentle quip, grounded in real-world experience, for every occasion. Though much of his humor was mildly political, it was also completely bipartisan, expressed with the gentleman's gift of not offending others, and reflecting an American consensus that politicians weren't to be trusted and that America's ideals were sound. He stood for the American values of enterprise, hard work, independence, and a healthy distrust of political rhetoric, which he thought was, for the most part, a lot of hot wind and hooey. He was a man of the real world and a patriot, not a theoretician or an agitator.

Rogers died tragically in a plane crash in Alaska in 1935. He was only fifty-five years old. He was survived by his widow, Betty Blake, and three of his four children. His son Will Rogers Jr. was briefly a congressman from California, though he resigned his seat to resume his commission in the United States Army, serving in World War II in General George S. Patton's Third Army, and winning the Bronze Star.

Will Rogers remains a beloved American legend and a true gentleman philosopher, whose homespun, cracker-barrel wisdom is as valuable now as it was to Americans of the last century.

RULE 7

BE READY TO EXIT THE OFFICE LIKE A GENTLEMAN

I thought of all my rotten jobs and how glad I was to have them, for a while.
Then it was a matter of quitting or getting fired. Both felt good.
—CHARLES BUKOWSKI

S ooner or later we all learn, often through personal experience, that even good people get fired. It isn't always fair how jobs and promotions are won or lost, but that's the way of the world, and the important thing is to focus on the next step.

That's why you need to be ready to exit your job with grace and dignity. Doing this the right way opens new doors and possibilities; doing this the wrong way burns bridges and hobbles potential.

I'll never forget my call from human resources. Another magazine editor and I were let go in a cost-cutting move. I was ready. I actually told the woman from human resources: "I'm sorry you have to make this call—it can't be easy." My manager told me he had fought for me, but I assured him he shouldn't worry. Before the week was out, I was given a column in the magazine and a commission to write a feature article. I still do contract work for the company. If I had lost my temper, I wouldn't have had these opportunities.

How we leave a job says more about us than how we start one. Walking into a new job can be challenging and even overwhelming, but it can also be exciting. Getting fired, on the other hand is traumatic, humbling, and humiliating. How you react to that says a lot about your character. It's no accident that some of the greatest political speeches have been farewells.

In the 2000 presidential election, Democratic nominee Al Gore had won the national popular vote, but an apparently narrow defeat in Florida gave Republican candidate George W. Bush a majority of delegates in the Electoral College.

Gore at first conceded defeat, but quickly reversed course, demanding a recount in Florida, and for weeks there was a rancorous political and legal wrangle as votes were recounted. The U.S. Supreme Court finally agreed to step in. The five conservative justices on the court sided with George W. Bush and the four liberal justices sided with Gore. The five to four ruling halted further recounting and let stand a declaration by Florida's secretary of state that Bush had won.

With the battle finally over, Al Gore appeared on national television to concede:

Good evening.

Just moments ago, I spoke with George W. Bush and congratulated him on becoming the 43rd President of the United States, and I promised him that I wouldn't call him back this time.

I offered to meet with him as soon as possible so that we can start to heal the divisions of the campaign and the contest through which we just passed.

Almost a century and a half ago, Senator Stephen Douglas told Abraham Lincoln, who had just defeated him for the presidency, "Partisan feeling must yield to patriotism. I'm with you, Mr. President, and God bless you."

Well, in that same spirit, I say to President-elect Bush that what remains of partisan rancor must now be put aside, and may God bless his stewardship of this country.

Neither he nor I anticipated this long and difficult road. Certainly neither of us wanted it to happen. Yet it came, and now it has ended, resolved, as it must be resolved, through the honored institutions of our democracy. [1]

However you feel about Gore, that was a gracious departure. He could have done anything after that.

Lou Gehrig's goodbye speech at Yankee Stadium remains the greatest farewell speech in sports. Gehrig had been diagnosed with the debilitating and fatal disease known as ALS (for amyotrophic lateral sclerosis). His tremendous baseball career had been cut short and he knew he would soon die a hard death, but Gehrig showed his appreciation to the fans in a humble and uplifting speech. He stood hat-in-hand before over sixty thousand fans in Yankees Stadium on July 4, 1939, and said in part:

> Fans, for the past two weeks you have been reading about the bad break I got. Yet today I consider myself the luckiest man on the face of the earth. I have been in ballparks for seventeen years and have never received anything but kindness and encouragement from you fans.
>
> Look at these grand men. Which of you wouldn't consider it the highlight of his career just to associate with them for even one day? Sure, I'm lucky.

In that stupendous moment Gehrig became immortal, an icon of what a man should be. He accepted his destiny, after giving life all he had, and he did so selflessly, with grace and respect for those who helped him along the way. Gehrig would die less than two years later.

Every man needs to be bigger than his setbacks. He needs to look to the future with confidence, and he should never allow himself to be downcast, angry, bitter, or vengeful. For the enterprising man, today's failure is tomorrow's opportunity. When Bernie Marcus and Arthur Blank, cofounders of Home Depot, were fired in April 1978, Marcus was fifty years old and Blank was thirty-five. They had lost out in a corporate power struggle at Handy Dan Home Improvement Centers. Handy Dan is long gone, but Marcus and Blank decided to open their own home-improvement store. Their first two Home Depot stores opened in Atlanta in 1979. You know what happened next.

Eleven Things You Should Do Immediately after Being Fired

I.   **Be prepared.** The call from human resources is rarely a total surprise.

2. **Don't lose your cool.** Instead, be magnanimous. Nothing will do more to wrong-foot your enemies, reassure your friends, and build corporate goodwill for you, than to leave your job with a kind word and a smile.

3. **Don't say anything rough.** You might be tempted to send an email ripping into management or telling off your boss or a coworker. Don't do it. You need to protect your reputation now more than ever. Keep your composure; be cordial, professional, and forward-looking, more interested in the next opportunity than settling scores about the past.

4. **Don't sign anything immediately.** Some companies offer severance payments in exchange for a "general release" in which you free them of any legal claims stemming from your employment. If you're offered this, don't sign right away. Look it over, and possibly run it by an attorney. You might be able to negotiate a better deal.

5. **Get references.** If possible—if, for instance, you've been let go because of budget cuts rather than fired for cause—get letters of recommendation from your former managers.

> **"**I didn't see it then, but it turned out that getting fired from Apple was the best thing that could have ever happened to me. The heaviness of being successful was replaced by the lightness of being a beginner again, less sure about everything. It freed me to enter one of the most creative periods of my life.**"**
> STEVE JOBS

Advice from the Office Gentleman
Never forget the grace of the Irish exit, otherwise known as leaving a party without saying goodbye. Don't pause or get roped into one last nightcap. Simply slip away—just send a thank-you note later.

6. **Look over your finances.** Cut out any unnecessary expenses and set yourself a realistic budget on which you can live for the next few months, while you look for a new job.

7. **File for unemployment.** In many states, fired employees can collect unemployment insurance.

8. **Take care of yourself.** If you've been putting off any health care appointments, make them now. You'll likely still have your employer's health care benefits until the end of the month. (You can also extend your coverage through the federal program COBRA.)

9. **Make a contact list.** Think about coworkers, clients, and vendors with whom you want to stay in touch. Reach out to them, and don't criticize your former employer or pose as a victim. Be upbeat and classy.

10. **See this as an opportunity.** This is a reset for your career or even a chance to do what you always wanted to do. Be realistic, but be confident too. If you felt stifled in your old job, you're no longer in a rut.

11. **Realize this is normal.** It is common for good, hard-working, and loyal people to lose their jobs. You haven't been cast out. You're setting off on a new adventure.

> " Not until we are lost do we begin to understand ourselves. "
>
> HENRY DAVID THOREAU

Why Cary Grant Gave Up Acting

Cary Grant starred in his last film *Walk, Don't Run* (1966) when he was sixty-two. He retired and resisted numerous attempts by Hollywood studios to coax him back onto the big screen. Grant realized that he had perfected himself as a character—people saw him in a certain role, and that role was as a sophisticated, middle-aged gentleman. He was embarrassed when critics panned him as a romantic partner for Audrey Hepburn in the otherwise terrific movie *Charade* (1963), because of their age differences. (He was fifty-nine and she was thirty-four). His next film, *Father Goose* (1964), cast him as an irascible old man, but he still got the girl, Leslie Caron who was thirty-three, while he was sixty. In *Walk, Don't Run*, he managed to avoid being the romantic lead, playing a British businessman (and matchmaker), in a light comedy that offered him a dignified exit from the movies. Gene Siskel, the movie critic, was one of the last people to interview Grant. When Siskel pointed out that Grant had earned himself a permanent place among the gods of the silver screen, Grant offered his final pronouncement on Hollywood. "I forgot to tell you," Grant said. "When you get off the trolley, you notice that it's been doing nothing but going around in circles. It doesn't go anywhere. You see the same things over and over. So you might as well get off."[2]

What a Man Says When It's Over

Now is the time to be the strong, silent type. Don't feel obligated to explain your reason for leaving a job and don't linger if you've been let go. Barring a non-compete clause in your contract or a situation where your current employer might want to make a counteroffer to a new opportunity you have, you don't have to give the company detailed reasons for your

> **Advice from the Office Gentleman**
> Sometimes it is better to step aside. After two terms in office as the first president of the United States, George Washington remained immensely popular, and could have been elected to a third term. Instead he chose to retire to his plantation home at Mount Vernon, and thereby gave America its first peaceful transition of power from one president to another.

departure. What you need to do is leave politely, with grace and dignity. If you do feel the need to offer parting advice, keep it uplifting and impersonal. Don't leave your employer in a bind even if they deserve it. You don't have to stay longer than two weeks, but in some cases that might be the right thing to do. When I gave notice at one magazine, they tried to get me to stay on for six weeks to finish a project on which I was the lead editor. Instead, I negotiated doing the work as a contractor, while I started the new job. (I cleared this arrangement with my new boss first of course.) It was a solution that satisfied all parties.

When to Ask for a Raise

The best time to get a raise is when you're switching jobs. You have more leverage when you're negotiating a new job—more than you're likely to ever have again with that employer. Employers also *expect* you to negotiate at this time, so not doing so means you are likely leaving money on the table.

If you don't want to look for a new job, but think you deserve more at your current one, the best time to negotiate a pay raise is during your annual review or when your job duties change. Be prepared when you go into these conversations. Your manager wants to stay on budget and he or she will look better to their superiors if they give you less. Go in after doing some analysis of what others in competing companies are making. Glassdoor.com and PayScale.com are great tools for getting this information.

Don't threaten or use another job offer to push for a raise. An employer will likely question the loyalty of anyone who plays that game. If you are serious about taking another job, you can and should ask your current employer to beat or match an offer. If you do that, make it clear you want to stay but that you have to take care of your family. They'll understand that.

How a Man Negotiates a Salary

When you negotiate a salary, try to maneuver your potential employer into making the first move by asking for the compensation range he has in mind. That can save you both a lot of time.

If possible, have this conversation in person. Often, though, you'll have to do it by phone—and if you do, use a landline so that there are no embarrassing glitches on the call because of a weak signal. Make sure your tone is positive, friendly, and strong.

Keep Tabs on Your Value

If you don't know what others are making who are doing similar work, you won't know if you're being paid a fair wage. Not knowing this information also can cause you to miss opportunities. If you keep an eye on the market and completely understand where you are in it then you can begin to see opportunities for advancement in similar fields or in new areas. This knowledge will also tell you when you need to develop new skills or credentials to make yourself more competitive. Remember, your goal in the workplace is to keep increasing your value; perpetual self-improvement isn't an option, it's a necessity.

Don't be rude if the offer is crazy low and don't leap like you won the lottery if it's higher than expected. Employers like to see enthusiasm, but it's perfectly acceptable to say that the offer sounds great, but that you'd like a day to think about it. If it's not even in the ballpark you can decline the offer now, but even as you do so, be polite and mature and keep the door open to future offers. There is no reason to burn a bridge; the employer might even be willing to expand the job and renegotiate the salary. If an offer is close to what you're looking for, emphasize the unique skills you bring and how you can benefit the company, and then make a counteroffer. It shouldn't be a made-up number; it needs to be a realistic number based on the market and your real worth. If the salary is set in stone, but the employer really wants you—and you really want the job—you can try to negotiate other types of compensation, including the amount of paid vacation time or offsite working opportunities that might be available to you, and you can ask about company standards for annual raises and bonuses.

Should You Tell a Prospective Employer Your Salary History?

Some states and municipalities, including California, Massachusetts, and New York City, have barred employers from asking for your salary history. Even if you are applying for a job in a location where the question is legal, you probably shouldn't answer this question. An honest evasion is better. Say something like: "Well, before trying to answer that we need an apples-to-apples comparison, as my current or former employer also gave these benefits, so what is it you offer?" If pressed, you can say something like: "I'd first like to say that I'm looking for $X." If you have moved, or would for the new job, you can stall by stating that the cost of living expenses is very different in the two locations.

What a Gentleman Doesn't Do in an Interview

1.   **Don't Fail to Prepare.** You get confidence from competence, so prepare. Study the company and write out why your skills are a good fit for its business. Writing this out will force you to think it out. Then, with a spouse or someone else you trust, do a mock interview to help you prepare. As you get ready, make sure you know enough about the company to be able to discuss various aspects of its business.

2.   **Don't Neglect Researching Your Interviewer.** If possible, go into the interview prepared with background information on the person interviewing you and the person who will be your supervisor. You might find a shared interest or connection that will build a bond.

3.   **Don't Wear Something Inappropriate.** It's better to be too formal (a tie) than too casual (a t-shirt), no matter what the job, and be conservative rather than flashy.

4.   **Don't Be Late.** You should be ten minutes early. That's it. If you are earlier than that then wait outside until ten minutes before. It's actually rude to show up too early.

5.   **Don't Look at Your Cell Phone.** Even if it keeps buzzing in your pocket, don't even glance at the device during the interview.

Advice from the Office Gentleman

The best and manliest way to erase a mistake during an interview is to pause, smile, and say that whatever you said came out wrong. Laugh at yourself, be honest, and be confident.

6. **Don't Ask Questions That Have Obvious Answers.** You should already know the basic info about the company and you'll sound unprepared if you ask questions that could be answered by looking at the company's website.

7. **Don't Badmouth Former Employers.** Saying something bad about a current or past employer just sounds rotten. Don't do it.

8. **Don't Get Too Personal.** Be friendly and open, but don't talk about your mother's cancer or your kid's school play.

9. **Don't Bring Up Salary Too Soon.** Bringing this up too soon puts you in a weaker negotiating position. It's better if they bring it up and make an offer first.

10. **Don't Have Poor Body Language.** Your body is always talking. Sit up straight but be relaxed and open. Don't fidget. Don't take a submissive posture by looking down or slouching. Be open and assertive.

11. **Don't Lie.** Being dishonest is always a bad idea. If the possible employer finds out you lied then you probably won't get the job, even if the fib is small.

12. **Don't Fail to Sell Yourself.** Don't be too humble, but don't be an arrogant ass either. Be ready with all you've done and frame it in a way that highlights what you can do for a new employer.

13. **Don't Make It All about You.** What you say should focus on how the company will benefit from hiring you.

THE FORTY-SEVEN RONIN

It is difficult to know yourself if you do not know others. To all Ways there are side-tracks. If you study a Way daily, and your spirit diverges, you may think you are obeying a good way, but objectively it is not the true Way. If you are following the true Way and diverge a little, this will later become a large divergence. You must realize this.

—MIYAMOTO MUSASHI, *THE BOOK OF FIVE RINGS*

On the site of the Shengakuji Temple in Tokyo, there is a museum near where the forty-seven *rōnin* (samurai with no lord or master) are buried. In this museum is a small display case that is centrally located but easy to overlook. Other display cases have samurai swords, helmets, and armor in them that attract the most attention. This small display case only has a parchment with the signatures of all forty-seven *rōnin* on it. Above the signatures is a small list, as this paper is actually a receipt. The receipt, which was left on the site by the *rōnin*, simply lists the things they took from the house in 1703, including one section of cloth and one head.

Yes, the forty-seven *rōnin* actually left a receipt for the head of the man they plotted to kill—and finally did kill, even though they knew that meant a death sentence for themselves.

In 1701 Asano Takumi-no-Kami Naganori, a *daimyō* (feudal lord), had been ordered to arrange a fitting reception for the envoy of the emperor in Edo (Tokyo). Kira Kozuke-no-Suke Yoshinaka, a powerful Edo official, was ordered to show Naganori how to do this. Kira was arrogant and insulted Naganori, whom he viewed as a rival, to goad him into drawing his sword. Kira knew that an attack on the envoy of the emperor was viewed as an attack on the emperor himself. Others say Kira wanted bribes that Naganori, a devout Confucian, wouldn't grant.

Naganori only managed to cut Kira's cheek before bystanders intervened and stopped the attack.

Naganori was then ordered to commit seppuku (ritual suicide) for striking a member of the court. Naganori's property was confiscated, his family ruined, and his samurai left leaderless—making them *rōnin*.

Naganori killed himself, as honor dictated, but then Ōishi Kuranosuke (also known as Oishi Yoshio), his top-ranking samurai, secretly vowed revenge. He was joined by a group of *rōnin* who later became popularly known as the "forty-seven *rōnin*."

Oishi began to frequent *geisha* houses, was seen drunk in public, and acted very obscenely to make it appear that he was a poor samurai who would not seek revenge; meanwhile, the rest of the faithful *rōnin* gathered in Edo. Some took jobs as workmen and merchants to gain access to Kira's house. One of the *rōnin* (Okano Kinemon Kanehide) even married the daughter of the builder of the house to obtain the plans. Others gathered weapons and secretly transported them to Edo.

In January 1703 Ōishi, with forty-six other *rōnin*, attacked Kira at his residence in Edo. After a long battle, they found Kira hiding and cut off his head.

After placing Kira's head on Naganori's grave, they surrendered. Ōishi and the other *rōnin* were sentenced to commit seppuku. Their graves are at the Shengakuji Temple. They are still revered in Japan as men who stood up for and fought for what they believed in.

14. **Have Questions Ready.** Most interviews finish with the person asking if you have any questions for them. Think about this beforehand and be ready with a few smart questions.

15. **Don't Flub the Question about Your Biggest Weakness.** Have a thoughtful, honest answer to this question that isn't self-destructive but that shows you are thoughtful and self-aware.

16. **Don't Go On and On.** Be friendly and easy to talk to, but don't talk so long you bore them.

17. **Don't Neglect to Ask about Next Steps.** Near the end of the interview, ask what comes next. Some will do several interviews, or maybe they'll want you to meet more members of the team.

18. **Don't Post Anything on Social Media.** Don't post anything about your interview on social media. This can tip off your current employer or end up embarrassing you if you don't get the job.

Follow Up after the Interview

The interview doesn't end when you leave the room or hang up the phone. How you follow up can make a big impression. Send a timely thank you note. Email is fine, because it's fast; but a quickly posted handwritten note always impresses. Remember employers are busy people and can easily get distracted by other aspects of their job, so it's all right to check in with them again after a couple of weeks, if you haven't heard anything. They might even appreciate the prodding.

AFTERWORD

THIS IS THE ULTIMATE BUSINESS GUIDEBOOK

BY GREG STUBE

Today's workplace is a battlefield. Your life might not be at risk, but your livelihood sure is. With this in mind, when I cracked open *The Ultimate Man's Survival Guide to the Workplace* I wasn't surprised to find it to be an essential primer for navigating the nine-to-five world, as the author helped me with my own book, *Conquer Anything: A Green Beret's Guide to Building Your A-Team*. What surprised me was how much I wished I had this book when I first entered the Army.

This book cuts out the business-school speak and tells you what you really need to know to make it in any company or bureaucracy—and the Army is certainly a bureaucracy. To clarify why I think this is such an important guidebook, I'd like to tell you a little about what I learned in the Green Berets and, more important, what I learned during the year I spent in the hospital recovering from wounds I received on the battlefield.

First of all, I wish I really had, as Miniter points out in "Rule 1," understand the rules of the new game. I had been in the Army eighteen years when I volunteered for Operation Medusa in late August 2006, a mission every American should know about, but so few do.

In hindsight I can still see myself striding across that base in Kandahar, on my way to volunteer for the mission. I wish I could go back there and slap some sense into myself. I am not saying I regret serving or even volunteering for that mission. I would do all that again. What I would like to do is shatter the arrogant self-image I had of myself at the time. My ego was blinding me to who I really needed to become; it was even causing me to treat others with disrespect just because they hadn't done what I had chosen to do.

Back then I was like an actor who immerses himself in a part, only I wasn't aware I was doing this. I was completely in step with the Green Beret ideal. I was a badass Special Forces soldier fighting for good and I let that warrior persona define me, even put blinders on me. Playing a role is important in any job we do, as it allows us to have clarity of mind so we can do the right thing even in difficult circumstances. But if you don't realize you are playing a part, then you are in danger of becoming a parody. Instead, you need your mind open so you can learn the rules of the workplace you're in, so that you can see and understand those around you, and so that you can challenge a bad rule or a bad person when necessary. We've all dealt with people who just can't do this—the secretary who won't even consider changing a protocol, a state employee at a motor-vehicle bureau who behaves as if they are a robot when you just need them to be human for a moment.

When I volunteered for that mission in Afghanistan in 2006, I was good at playing my part and contributing, but arrogance has a way of blinding you, especially when you've seen so many things all those people back home don't know anything about, not really. You know this and it makes you conceited.

So when I look back at my Green Beret persona before Operation Medusa and all that would come after, I know how right I was about a lot of it but how blind I was too. My clean adherence to what a Green Beret should be actually became a weakness. The complete devotion to this ideal is even part of the reason why so many of our returning soldiers have a hard time recovering from post-traumatic stress disorder (PTSD).

Entering a workplace is like this too—well, without the life-or-death part. I've been in the private sector more than a decade now. In that time I've forced myself to look around, not to judge but to learn. A leader must have enough control of his ego to do that.

I learned the hard way that this book's "Rule 2: A Man's Image Must Not Be a Work of Fiction" is so important to understand.

During a multi-day battle with an estimated one thousand Taliban fighters, I was blown up in a maneuvering Humvee and then shot multiple times and badly burned before I was rescued and somehow medivacked out. No one thought I would live. Expert medical care from a Green Beret medic kept me alive. I was transported to Germany and then to a burn unit in San Antonio, Texas. At each step the doctors expected me to die at any time.

Finally, there I was in the burn unit and on life support. You sure think about a lot of things when you're in a hospital bed with tubes in you and pieces of your body sewn back on, all the while knowing you really should be dead. At first, how you judge yourself is the worst of it. I was a Green Beret with eighteen years of experience and I was physically tough and had skills

I was proud of, earned in sweat and blood. Then I found I'd only worked to harden the parts that were blown up and burned away. I found that everything I needed to really be strong was undeveloped and little understood and that mainstream society and even the Army didn't grasp any of this.

Answers are fleeting in those early and agonizing hours. I was charred and stitched back together and no one could then say if I'd live or die. Machines were beeping along with my vital signs. I was gagging on the smell of my burned flesh. I was as helpless and as close to death as a newborn conceived prematurely. I was flat on my back and couldn't see my feet and hoped they were still there. When the nurses turned the lights off at night, I'd lie looking up into the dark and wonder if I'd be better off dead.

Then I realized that wasn't the worst of it.

The first to come to the hospital was my wife. She came into my hospital room in San Antonio just a day after I'd arrived and after the first of dozens of surgeries. She had a white gown over her clothes and a white cap over her hair and a white facemask covering her mouth and nose. My wounds were so fresh and open anything could infect me so everyone wore these things before they came into my private room.

When she walked in, I looked across the room and into her brown eyes. They were moist and wide and were expanding from gut-wrenching horror and then she was falling, falling forward. I tried to reach for her. I couldn't move. My left arm tried to go up. My torso tried to sit up. None of that was possible. I fell back with pain smashing through my convulsing body as she landed facedown on the tile floor with a fleshy thud. This was a preview of coming attractions, as I wouldn't be helping anyone for a long time, not even myself.

Pain crashed through me like jolts of electricity. The torment that I couldn't help my wife rattled me deep below where the flesh hurts. I couldn't even help her off the floor. I wasn't a man anymore. I was just some destroyed piece of flesh lying on white sheets.

She was out cold and face down on the tile floor and no nurse even noticed. I called out and the heaving of my chest and gut almost made me pass out. I frantically tapped the call button with my right index finger for a nurse and it seemed forever before anyone responded. Time went so slowly. I was dying inside knowing she was down there and I couldn't do a damn thing about it.

Finally, a nurse came into the room and helped my wife off the floor. She took her from the room by holding her right arm and waist as someone does for a very drunk person.

She knew what happened but nothing could prepare her for how I looked. Part of my abdomen was so swollen that it was on a table pushed up to the edge of my bed. I was covered in bandages. I still had my legs and arms but one of my legs had to be virtually sewn back on, as the fracture was so complete and compound.

I'll never forget the cryptic conversation my father had with the head surgeon not long after this as I lay on the hospital bed.

The doctor said to my father, "Sir, your son has lost a lot of intestines."

My dad said, "That's good."

I managed to say through the pain and drugs they were pumping into me, "That's not good."

My father looked at my swollen midsection, at where a piece of shrapnel four inches wide had been taken out of me, and said, "Look at it this way, son, now you don't have the guts to go back to Afghanistan."

This was so much the right thing to say. I wanted to laugh, but it hurt too much.

Looking back I'd say that my father knew from experience how to act. He'd been badly burned while serving in the Navy. He was the only one to survive a horrifying accident on a ship. During the Vietnam War an ensign had flipped the wrong switch near a jet engine. Hydraulic fluid sprayed everyone. It lit on fire and became a flamethrower. Five people died almost instantly. When my father stood up, his palms stuck to the metal deck and the skin from his elbows to his fingertips slid off like rubber gloves. Medics tried to help him, but he pushed them away with his skinless hands. He kept fighting them off as he walked to sickbay.

When he walked into sickbay, there was this young medic there and my father said, "Hey kid, you got a Band-Aid?"

My father never told me that story. I heard it from another Navy man who'd seen the whole thing. That was how my dad lived. He was Chief Stube to the day he died. Though my dad was medically discharged from the Navy after that accident, he reentered the U.S. military later and completed nearly thirty years of service for his country.

As we talked my father reminded me that George Washington is on the Purple Heart. Washington, that man, that general, our first president who stood up bravely under fire so many times and who kept the course for freedom as his army starved and struggled to even find enough boots during harsh winters at Valley Forge, is on the Purple Heart. He explained that Washington didn't want to be president and that he willingly left the White House and peacefully passed the reins of power after just two terms—setting an example of what someone who believes in things greater than himself does.

Still, at this desperate hour I was sinking, falling into an abyss of being nothing I knew anymore. I was a dead body that was somehow still awake and was screaming in my head that I shouldn't be here. I should be under a gravestone in Arlington that my wife and, someday, son could put flowers next to on Memorial Day weekends as they called me a hero and shed a tear before moving on with their lives.

I thought on this as I looked up at that bare hospital ceiling and smelled my burned flesh. I realized I couldn't even come up with a good definition of what a hero was, so how did I know I even was one or if they would even think of me that way. All I knew was whatever I had been was blown away and I honestly couldn't even define what I had lost, aside from the physical things. If I couldn't define what was lost, how could I get back on my feet?

The image of the indestructible warrior I'd long lived by was dead. I felt dead. I felt like I was a corpse and that my spirit was floating around the room and seeing all these unseeing people and wondering why they didn't see me.

I was just beginning to understand that people aren't whole who live like I had for all those years. I was starting to understand how shallow I'd been.

I was beginning to see there are two halves to what makes a person whole, to complete a real code for success in life. It would take a lot more pain and trouble before I would understand any of this.

Meanwhile, the Army's attempt to give us continuity was to assign us case managers. These were basically social workers. They understood the bureaucratic process, but not what really mattered. They treated me like I was a child. I was a senior non-commissioned officer in the Special Forces with more schooling and leadership experience than they'd ever see, but they were treating me like some abused child who is now a ward of the state. I couldn't break through their superficial and very bureaucratic point of view. To them I was just another one of those wounded men they had to deal with. They wouldn't look me in the eyes or try to see me for who I was. They absolutely refused to give me credit for anything I might have done before becoming a professional patient. This infuriated me. I'd seldom witnessed this kind of condescension, even as a buck private in the infantry. Some thought of themselves as some kind of parole officers, gladly scaling back my freedoms. What a god complex.

Then one day my wife Donna and I saw the wife of another wounded soldier. She was walking from our quarters to the hospital across the street. She was wearing pajamas. We both criticized her lack of decorum. We thought she should keep a better appearance for her wounded husband and for the military community. But then we found out that her husband had died of his wounds and that she had come running from bed. She was so distraught that what she was wearing didn't matter.

We fell apart when we learned this. We detested ourselves for thinking such judgmental things. How dare we judge her? How did we know what she'd gone through, who she was, and what was happening? We were thinking just as superficially as the bureaucratic caseworkers.

This was when we turned a corner together. This was when faith began to heal us.

Donna and I both made a conscious effort to stop judging others and ourselves superficially. This new way of seeing things made me begin to hate the phrase "wounded warrior." I get it. It's graphic and real. Some of our warriors come back with parts missing and with holes shot right through them. But that's just their body, not them. When I learned to suspend judgment and open my eyes to the truth that there is something in us and that something is more important than our bodies, I began to heal. It took all but losing my body for me to understand this. All of what happened to me and what was killing those around me settled into a theme that suddenly showed what I needed and what anyone who gets lost in war or in life really needs.

The code I'd lived my life by as a Green Beret soldier was no longer enough. I needed these deeper, what I call feminine virtues, to become a complete person who could climb out of that hospital bed and create new A-Teams to tackle the next physical and mental challenges in my personal and professional life. Miniter is right, we have to define ourselves by who we are, not by some fiction we are trying to personify.

It is so important that this book's next rule—Be a Man of Action in the Workplace—depends on it. The need to be a man of action is clearer in the military, but it is no less important in the American workplace.

While serving as cadre at the John F. Kennedy Special Warfare Center and School, I had a student named Riley Stephens. I didn't like him. Personally and professionally, I saw nothing of value in him. I simply judged him harshly and felt very negatively about him. To my great relief, Staff Sergeant Stephens failed to meet the standards in training. He was not a man of action. My recommendation was NTR, or Never to Return. I felt so strong in my dislike for him that I couldn't picture how he had made it as far in training as he did. I even felt as though my own Green Beret would have less value if he got one.

I told him when he left that my own dad would be pissed if I passed someone who wouldn't be able to save my bacon in combat. Apparently, he had done well after that, because he received strong recommendations to return to Special Forces' candidacy. In the meantime, I had left my instructor position to rejoin a combat unit and was in no position to object.

This Stephens guy went through that tough training all over again. This time he passed. I found out because we were later on an A-Team together— during that big mission when I was wounded.

The real wakeup call with Riley Stephens came when I was lying on the battlefield—and dying—surrounded by guys who couldn't possibly save my life. They kept telling me to hang on, that the medic was on the way. Don't get me wrong, I had some great and heroic help, but not the kind that could actually save my life, given the condition I was in. As I lay dying, they said, "Here he is, Stube!" Then I saw the medic running up to my feet with that big aid bag. It was Riley Stephens.

My pain was horrible, like nothing I'd ever imagined. The traumatic damage and burns were almost unbearable. Yet, when I saw Riley, these words came quickly: "No hard feelings, right, Stephens?"

His eyes were wide open with concern and professionalism as he performed a rapid trauma assessment on me. It was clear that he wanted so badly to save my life. It was also clear that he wanted to prove to me that he could do this now—when it counted. He could save my bacon. Riley hit all the marks of a flawless trauma clinic, stopping hard to reach hemorrhaging in multiple places, dressing burns, and so much more. He had become a better medic than I was, and for the first time, I could feel pride in it. Before my own life was on the line, it would have been an insult for me to think that a student could be better than I was. What an ego. Now I know that it is necessary that we give everything we have to the next generation. If they are not better than we are, then we are failing. Yet another example of how I needed this to get the chip off my shoulder.

Though I should have been long unconscious by that time, I had the blessing and the curse of being fully aware of everything happening. As a Special Forces medic, I was very concerned with how everything was being done. And then, as he worked, I remember feeling like I didn't need to worry anymore. I saw that he had firm command over my survivability. He and the good Lord both had hands on me that day.

As I witnessed my teammates and commander clearly upset by my condition, I started feeling upset too. I was getting indicators that they thought I would surely die. Taking a page out of Chief Stube's playbook, I tried to get Riley's attention as my teammates carried me on the litter toward the medevac

Blackhawk two hours after I'd been hit. I couldn't speak up loudly, so I reached up toward Riley, who was at my right shoulder. As I reached toward him and strained to speak his name over the noise of the battle and the helicopter there to take me out of the battlefield, he noticed my effort. Immediately, Riley screamed out to the crew with a true sense of urgency, "Put him down easy. Now!" As the litter touched the ground, there was a whole team of heads looking over me to see what was wrong. I used all the strength I had to speak up. "Riley, when I get…back…to Kandahar…I'm …telling everyone…you…touched…my…penis!"

I think it worked. I could see humor and relief in everyone. Riley seemed on the verge of tears, though, as he said something like, "Stube, you son of a bitch…"

I just couldn't stand the thought of everyone being down, even if I *was* going to die. The guys hoisted me up once more and marched me toward the noise and the rotor wash of my green chariot. To Kandahar I went, but in my mind it was to the unknown.

I saw Riley back at Fort Bragg a few months later, when I got a pass from the hospital to go home for a few days. When he stood before me, all I could do was cry. I was overwhelmed with gratitude and guilt. So grateful for how he worked to save my life, and so guilty for the way I had judged him and cast him away. I also felt guilty that friends we shared had been killed, but I survived. Riley hated to see me broken like that, and he quickly wrote his name and number on a Post-it Note to hand to me. He put his hand on my shoulder firmly and walked away. He was saving me from the embarrassment of crying, and it also seemed that he had a hard time dealing with it.

I put the note on my computer monitor at home, and made firm plans to be in touch with him. Riley Stephens had gone from being a man I despised to someone on my permanent Christmas card list. Still, a couple years later I had not called him. I did not send a Christmas card. I had not taken my son to be around Riley Stephens. While I had been focused on myself, my recovery, and my new life after the military, Riley had been back in combat multiple times. I was still thinking of myself when the call came that Riley had been killed in

Afghanistan. The medic on scene could not save him. My considerations for building and maintaining a team changed in that moment. How could I have been so selfish?

Riley showed even people who don't look the type can be men of action when needed. Miniter is right about this and so much more. His detailed advice, some gleaned from interviews with many notable professionals from many fields, is *the* guidebook to all you need to know to succeed in the battlefield that is today's workplace.

APPENDICES

CONTINUE YOUR MANLY EDUCATION

APPENDIX 1

50 Books Every Businessman Should Read

1. *The Bible,* Proverbs: You might be surprised at how much wisdom is to be found in this ancient book of the Bible, and how relevant it is to your life in and out of the office.

2. *The Cost of Discipleship* by Dietrich Bonhoeffer, 1937: A classic treatise on the Christian call to self-sacrifice—by a man who lived it.

3. *In Search of Excellence* by Thomas Peters, 1982: An essential business book, full of real-life lessons.

4. *The Short, Happy Life of Francis Macomber* by Ernest Hemingway, 1936: Maintaining courage under pressure is a manly trait—and no one expressed it better than Ernest Hemingway.

5. *Gentleman: A Timeless Fashion* by Bernhard Roetzel, 1999: A sophisticated man's guide to style and dress.

6. *The Hero with a Thousand Faces* by Joseph Campbell, 1949: One of the most influential books of the 20th century, and one that can put your own life's journey into context.

7. *Clothes and the Man: The Principles of Fine Men's Dress* by Alan Flusser, 1985: An illustrative guide on how a man should shape his image to succeed.

8. *Barbarians at the Gate* by Bryan Burrough and John Helyar, 1989: An astounding work of investigative journalism that details the greed, politics, and stupidity that led to the leveraged buyout of RJR Nabisco.

9. *Conquer Anything* by Greg Stube, 2018: A Green Beret offers hard-earned lessons on team leadership.

10. *Zen in the Art of Archery* by Eugen Herrigel, 1948: Zen is an often-misunderstood concept in the West. Herrigel spent years in Japan learning the art of Zen through archery, and in the process teaches ways to simplify and perfect how we pursue our goals.

11. *Never Eat Alone* by Keith Ferrazzi, 2005: Ferrazzi emphasizes that business is about relationships, and why your lunch hour shouldn't be wasted time.

12. *Death in the Afternoon* by Ernest Hemingway, 1932: This is a book on bullfighting, but also about a man's code, the necessity of courage, and life's inevitable tragedy.

13. *The Bonfire of the Vanities* by Tom Wolfe, 1987: A satirical novel about how even a financial "master of the universe" can find himself at the mercy of fate.

14. *12 Rules for Life: An Antidote to Chaos* by Jordan Peterson, 2008: A self-improvement book that's also an intellectual tour de force.

15. *The Ultimate Man's Survival Guide* by Frank Miniter, 2009: This book's older brother, a guide to attaining all the skills a man must master.

16. *Goodbye, Darkness: A Memoir of the Pacific War* by William Manchester, 1980: A memoir of a Marine's service in the Pacific theatre during World War II, and the lessons it taught.

17. *How to Win Friends and Influence People* by Dale Carnegie, 1936: One of the best-selling self-help books of all time—and with good reason.

18. *The Quick and Easy Way to Effective Speaking* by Dale Carnegie, 1962: Public speaking is storytelling—and Carnegie shows you how to do it.

19. *A Rumor of War* by Philip Caputo, 1977: This classic Vietnam War memoir is a lesson in growing up, in seeing the world for what it is, and not being defeated by all it throws at you.

20. *American Caesar* by William Manchester, 1978: This biography of General Douglas MacArthur reads like a novel about an ambitious man, a man who did more in one lifetime than most of us can even dream of achieving.

21. *Washington: A Life* by Ron Chernow, 2010: A study of the greatest leader in American history.

22. *Robert E. Lee on Leadership: Executive Lessons in Character, Courage, and Vision* by H.W. Crocker, 2000: Lee is still deeply loved in the South. He led with a quiet charisma all of us can learn from.

23. *The Index Card* by Helen Olen and Harold Pollack, 2016: This is a must read for guys who want to learn how to invest. Pollack is an economist who mentioned on a talk show that he could put the ten most important rules of investing on a 3x5 card. After being hounded for not posting it, he finally did and it went viral.

24. *Dark Age Ahead* by Jane Jacobs, 2004: Jacobs—author of *The Death and Life of Great American Cities* and *The Economy of Cities*—pinpoints the pillars of our culture that are in decay, such as family, higher education, and the effective practice of science, and argues that the erosion of these things is leading to environmental crisis, racism, and the growing gulf between rich and poor. This book is a way for anyone in business to see and get ready for what's coming.

25. *Meditations* by Marcus Aurelius: Marcus Aurelius, a Roman emperor, was a philosopher-king. His *Meditations*, meant to be an exercise in self-improvement, have spoken to countless generations about the virtues of stoicism.

26. *The Crowd: A Study of the Popular Mind* by Gustave Le Bon, 1895: This insightful book offers insights that any leader can understand. For instance, "The masses have never thirsted after the truth. Whoever can supply them with illusions is easily their master; whoever attempts to destroy their illusions is always their victim."

27. *The Economist: Megachange: The World in 2050*, edited by Daniel Franklin and John Andrews, 2012: Provocative essays about the "megachanges" that will be shaping our future.

28. *The Elements of Style* by William Strunk and E.B. White, 1918: Business is about communicating, and this is the best book ever written on how to communicate with the written word.

29. *How to Have Confidence and Power in Dealing with People* by Leslie T. Giblin, 1956: This book shows how to deal with people as they really are, not how you think or wish they were.

30. *Endurance: Shackleton's Incredibly Voyage* by Alfred Lansing, 1959: This is the story of one of the most traumatic seafaring adventures gone wrong. Lansing shows how the polar explorer Ernest Shackleton finally led his sailors back to civilization.

31. *Good to Great: Why Some Companies Make the Leap…and Others Don't* by Jim Collins, 2001: Collins reveals the leadership skills that bring companies long-term success.

32. *Primal Leadership: Learning to Lead with Emotional Intelligence* by Daniel Goleman, Richard E. Boyatzis, and Annie McKee, 2001: This book shows how great leaders use characteristics like empathy and self-awareness to get great results.

33. *The Seven Habits of Highly Effective People* by Stephen R. Covey, 1989: Adopt these habits—and see how they change your life for the better.

34. *The Art of War* by Sun Tzu: War and business have more in common than you might think; this ancient Chinese text is a masterclass in strategy.

35. *Developing the Leader Within You* by John C. Maxwell, 1993: Every manager is a leader, and this a very useful book for honing your leadership talents.

36. *Influence: The Psychology of Persuasion* by Robert Cialdini, 1984: After 35 years of behavioral research, Dr. Robert Cialdini explains the psychology behind getting people to say "yes."

37. *Team of Rivals: The Political Genius of Abraham Lincoln* by Doris Kearns Goodwin, 2005: This biographical account of Abraham Lincoln and his cabinet sheds light on the president's leadership style, his understanding of human behavior, and the way he reconciled conflicting personalities and political factions.

38. *The Alchemist* by Paulo Coelho, 1988: A timeless fable about listening to your heart and staying true to your dreams.

39. *Liar's Poker* by Michael Lewis, 1989: An entertaining and instructive memoir of the author's days as a bond salesman in the 1980s.

40. *True North: Discover Your Authentic Leadership* by Bill George and Peter Sims, 2007: A step by step plan to become a successful leader—strongly sourced with 125 top leader interviews.

41. *Strengths Based Leadership: Great Leaders, Teams, and Why People Follow* by Tom Rath and Barrie Conchie, 2008: With Gallup surveys, interviews, and first-hand accounts from successful CEOs, this book has great advice for becoming a better leader.

42. *The Ascent of Money: A Financial History of the World* by Niall Ferguson, 2008: A history of the world's financial system, from ancient Mesopotamia to today, explaining why credit and debt is as important as technological innovation to economic success.

43. *Switch: How to Change Things When Change Is Hard* by Chip and Dan Heath, 2010: With stories from everyday leaders, this book teaches how to overcome obstacles to achieve transformative change.

44. *The Truth About Leadership: The No-fads, Heart-of-the-Matter Facts You Need to Know* by James M. Kouzes and

Barry Z. Posner, 2010: Based on 30 years of research of tried-and-true tactics from around the world, Kouzes and Posner dive into what's at the very core of effective leadership.

45. *On Becoming a Leader* by Warren Bennis, 1989: This thought-provoking classic of business literature draws from hundreds of interviews to help answer the question: What makes a good leader?

46. *Turn the Ship Around* by L. David Marquet, 2012: This is a powerful book on leadership by a former commander of a U.S. Navy submarine.

47. *The War of Art* by Steven Pressfield, 2002: This fun to read, insightful little book shows how to overcome your inner demons to achieve your dreams.

48. *Man's Search for Meaning* by Viktor Frankl, 1946: This book chronicles Frankl's experiences as an Auschwitz concentration camp inmate, and how he made sense of and overcame incredible suffering.

49. *Tribes: We Need You to Lead Us* by Seth Godin, 2008: This little book details how to form a team, a "tribe," that will unite for success.

50. *The Innovator's Dilemma* by Clayton Christensen, 1997: Christensen shows how even outstanding companies can do everything right, yet still lose market leadership if they fail to understand emerging technology.

APPENDIX II

50 Movies Every Businessman Should See

1. *Citizen Kane*, 1941, directed by Orson Welles: This heavily fictionalized biopic of William Randolph Hearst was written by and starred Orson Welles as "Charles Foster Kane," a man who rises from poverty (via the discovery of a gold mine on his family's property) to wealth and power, only to fall again.

2. *Wall Street*, 1987, directed by Oliver Stone: Gordon Gekko (Michael Douglas) is a Wall Street tycoon gone bad. Gekko's speech on greed is epic. He is a cliché of a character, but the movie is a cautionary tale about the worst side of American business.

3. *The Prisoner*, TV series, 1967: Patrick McGoohan stars as a British former secret agent who is abducted and imprisoned in a mysterious coastal village resort where his captors try to find out why he abruptly resigned from his job. This show was well before its time. It says a lot about corporate conformity, control, and surveillance.

4. *Dodsworth*, 1936, directed by William Wyler: Samuel Dodsworth (Walter Huston) retires from his auto empire and takes his much younger wife to Europe. She falls for several men in aristocratic circles in Europe. He sticks by her long after most would have filed for divorce. The film pits the American self-made man against the European man of inherited titles and wealth.

5. *Office Space,* 1999, directed by Mike Judge: This comedy satirizes the everyday work life of a typical mid-to-late-1990s software company, focusing on a handful of individuals fed up with their jobs.

6. *Boom Town,* 1940, directed by Jack Conway: "Big John" McMasters (Clark Gable) and "Square John" Sand (Spencer Tracy) are two down-on-their-luck oil wildcatters who join forces. They go broke and strike it rich multiple times as they fight over the same girl (Claudette Colbert). This politically incorrect movie couldn't be made today, but it is a fun, swashbuckling lesson in risk and reward.

7. *Barbarians at the Gate,* 1993, directed by Glenn Jordan: RJR Nabisco CEO F. Ross Johnson decides to take the tobacco and food conglomerate private in 1988 after receiving advance news of the likely market failure of the company's smokeless cigarette. The resulting fallout is a tale of corporate greed and avarice. It won both the Primetime Emmy Award for Outstanding Television Movie and the Golden Globe for Best Television Movie.

8. *Joy,* 2015, directed by David O. Russell: The true story (Hollywood style) of Joy Mangano, inventor, entrepreneur, and self-made millionaire.

9. *Boiler Room,* 2000, directed by Ben Younger: An entertaining business morality tale about a college dropout who becomes a phony stock investor.

10. *Casino*, 1995, directed by Martin Scorsese: Robert De Niro (Sam "Ace" Rothstein) is sent by the Chicago mob to oversee the day-to-day operations at the Tangiers Casino in Las Vegas. His character is based on Frank Rosenthal, who ran the Stardust, Fremont, and Hacienda casinos in Las Vegas for the Chicago Outfit from the 1970s until the early 1980s. Joe Pesci plays Nicholas "Nicky" Santoro, based on real-life Mob enforcer Anthony Spilotro, a man who could give Ace protection. The result is a fast-paced action drama and exploration of the dirty side of business.

11. *e-Dreams*, 2001, directed by Wonsuk Chin: This business documentary chronicles the rise and fall of Kozmo. com, and is a lesson about the dangers of fashionable business trends.

12. *Jobs*, 2013, directed by Joshua Michael Stern: This dramatic biography of Steve Jobs follows his rise to power as the founder of Apple.

13. *Moneyball*, 2011, directed by Bennett Miller: This is a classic underdog' story about how the small-budget Oakland Athletics used sophisticated sabermetric analyses of baseball players in order to compete and win on the cheap.

14. *Patton*, 1970, directed by Franklin J. Schaffner: This biography follows the life of General George S. Patton during World War II, illustrating both his great and inspiring leadership, and his undeniable faults.

15. *Peter Jones: How We Made Our Millions*, 2011, BBC: This documentary tries to discover the secret recipe to entrepreneurial success by interviewing some of Britain's leading entrepreneurs.

16. *A Christmas Carol*, 1938, directed by Edwin L. Marin: Ebenezer Scrooge learns a fundamental lesson: we must use our success to help others.

17. *Something Ventured*, 2011, directed by Daniel Geller and Dayna Goldfine: This documentary features a series of insightful interviews with some of America's most famous venture capitalists.

18. *Thank You for Smoking*, 2006, directed by Jason Reitman: This film explores the contradictions between selling a product well and not having a great product to sell. It's a fun and brilliant exploration of business communication and ethics.

19. *The Big Short*, 2015, directed by Adam McKay: Based on the book by Michael Lewis, the movie shows how a group of canny investors predicted and took advantage of the housing market bubble.

20. *The Founder*, 2016, directed by John Lee Hancock: A film about how Ray Kroc turned McDonald's into one of the most successful franchises of all time.

21. *The Men Who Built America*, 2012, The History Channel: This documentary explores the American Dream by following the lives and business stories of some of America's most innovative and influential businessmen.

22. *The Pursuit of Happyness*, 2006, directed by Gabriele Muccino: The true story of a man who went from homelessness to entrepreneurial success.

23. *The Social Network*, 2010, directed by David Fincher: This is the dramatic story of the founding and early massive success of Facebook.

24. *Too Big to Fail*, 2011, directed by Curtis Hanson: This HBO drama dives into the 2008 financial meltdown and its immediate aftermath.

25. *Trading Places*, 1983, directed by John Landis: Dan Aykroyd is Louis Winthorpe, a spoiled and prosperous commodities broker, and Eddie Murphy is Billy Ray Valentine, a homeless beggar and criminal. In a bet, two brothers who employ Winthorpe decide to perform a social experiment by switching him with Billy Ray. The fallout is surprising and funny.

26. *War Dogs*, 2016, directed by Todd Phillips: Two young Americans get involved with the international arms trade. Their venture grows quickly until they bid for a huge contract to supply the Afghanistan National Army. To fulfill the deal they end with up in a shady arrangement with wanted international arms dealers.

27. *Michael Clayton*, 2007, directed by Tony Gilroy: A searing drama about legal and corporate corruption.

28. *Glengarry Glen Ross*, 1992, directed by James Foley: This film was adapted by David Mamet from his 1984 Pulitzer Prize-winning play of the same name. It's a lesson in how *not* to motivate a team.

29. *The Apartment*, 1960, directed by Billy Wilder: *The Apartment* was controversial in its day for its frank depiction of infidelity. Jack Lemmon plays C.C. Baxter, a lonely office worker for a New York insurance company. Weak-willed and unambitious, Baxter allows company executives to use his apartment for meetings with their mistresses, in return for good personnel reports. When the personnel director catches on to the scheme, he blackmails Baxter for exclusive apartment privileges. Being a romantic comedy, love eventually wins out.

30. *Woman's World*, 1954, directed by Jean Negulesco: This film says a lot about corporate America in the 1950s. As three men compete for the top job at a large company, the company owner invites all three men and their wives to New York City so he can evaluate them. It turns into a corporate drama as the wives advise and lobby for their husbands. There is still a lot of truth in this tale.

31. The television series *Gunsmoke* (1955-1975), *Bonanza* (1959-1973), and *The Rifleman* (1958-1963) all presented strong cases for ethical and very manly leadership.

32. *A Man for All Seasons*, 1966, directed by Fred Zinnemann: A classic movie, winner of six Academy Awards, that tells the true story of how Sir Thomas More stayed to true to his conscience at the cost of his life.

33. *A Good Year*, 2006, directed by Ridley Scott: In this romantic comedy Russell Crowe is Max Skinner, a successful but selfish and lonely bond trader who inherits an estate in France. He soon has to decide between the pursuit of money and the pursuit of happiness.

34. *Up in the Air*, 2009, directed by Jason Reitman: George Clooney is Ryan Bingham, a corporate downsizer who ends up having to deal with the real lives he is shattering.

35. *Margin Call*, 2011, directed by J.C. Chandor: The principal story takes place over a tense, 24-hour period at a large Wall Street investment bank during the initial stages of the financial crisis of 2007-2008.

36. *Enron: The Smartest Guys in the Room*, 2005, directed by Alex Gibney: This documentary, based on a book of the same name, examines the 2001 collapse of the Enron Corporation, which resulted in criminal trials for several of the company executives; it also shows the involvement of the Enron traders in the California electricity crisis. It's an important discussion on the relationship between big business and big government.

37. *Other People's Money*, 1991, directed by Norman Jewison: This comedy follows Lawrence "Larry the

Liquidator" Garfield (Danny DeVito), a successful corporate raider who has made his fortune buying up companies and selling off their assets. With the help of a computerized stock analyzing program called "Carmen," he identifies New England Wire & Cable Company as his next target. The struggling company is run by Andrew "Jorgy" Jorgenson (Gregory Peck). What follows is a battle for control.

38. *Risky Business*, 1983, directed by Paul Brickman: Joel Goodson (Tom Cruise) is a wealthy high school student who finds himself desperately short of cash, and ends up raising it in a most unexpected (and not recommended) way.

39. *The Man in the Gray Flannel Suit*, 1956, directed by Nunnally Johnson: Tom Rath (Gregory Peck) is a young World War II veteran trying to balance his marriage and family life with the demands of a new job while dealing with the after-effects of his war service.

40. *Patterns*, 1956, directed by Fielder Cook: Van Heflin is Fred Staples, a corporate manager. He is promoted to a dream job in the big city, but he soon finds he is there to replace an original partner who has lost his edge. This sets up a dramatic conflict with his ruthless boss (Everett H. Sloane).

41. *The Best Years of Our Lives*, 1946, directed by William Wyler: In this classic drama three men return from

World War II. One has lost his hands. Another has returned to no job prospects and a cheating wife. The other returns to his old job at a bank but he is confused about his role in society—should he give any servicemen who needs money a loan? A tremendous drama about love, duty, and responsibility.

42. *The Strange Love of Martha Ivers*, 1946, directed by Lewis Milestone: Sam Masterson (Van Heflin) returns to his childhood town, a place he fled from in a box car. He finds his childhood friend Martha Ivers (Barbara Stanwyck) married to weakling Walter O'Neil (Kirk Douglas in his big-screen debut). Martha is the heir to a fortune and owner of a large factory in town. She wants Masterson to kill her husband and to take the helm.

43. *Paths of Glory*, 1957, directed by Stanley Kubrick: The film stars Kirk Douglas as Colonel Dax, who is outraged that soldiers from his regiment are being scapegoated for a failed attack. He defends his men in a court-martial, but it is a sham trial, and three of the men are ordered shot. Colonel Dax is then offered a promotion, which he angrily rejects. The film is a jarring portrayal of ruthless self-interest against honor and honesty.

44. *Pirates of Silicon Valley*, 1999, directed by Martyn Burke: Noah Wyle plays Steve Jobs and Anthony Michael Hall plays Bill Gates in this film. It spans the years

1971-1997 and is based on Paul Freiberger and Michael Swaine's 1984 book *Fire in the Valley: The Making of the Personal Computer*. It explores the impact of the rivalry between Jobs (Apple Computer) and Gates (Microsoft) on the development of the personal computer.

45. *Chasing Madoff*, 2010, directed by Jeff Prosserman: This film, based on a book by Harry Markopolos, follows a team of investigators as they work to uncover and expose a real-life Ponzi scheme that fleeced hundreds of people out of millions.

46. *Gone with the Wind*, 1939, directed by Victor Fleming: This epic film was adapted from Margaret Mitchell's 1936 Pulitzer Prize-winning novel of the same name. It is set in the American South against the backdrop of the American Civil War and the Reconstruction era, and tells the story of Scarlett O'Hara (Vivien Leigh), a strong-willed daughter of a Georgia plantation owner. She loses everything, but then with grit and ruthless determination she regains her position in society, only to be undone by faults in her character. It remains one of the all-time great movies.

47. *The Fountainhead*, 1949, directed by King Vidor: Based on Ayn Rand's novel, the movie stars Gary Cooper as Howard Roark, an architect who believes in pursuing his individual artistic vision regardless of the financial cost in order to retain his personal integrity.

48. *How the West Was Won*, 1962, directed by John Ford, Henry Hathaway, and George Marshall: Set between 1839 and 1889, this film follows four generations of

a family (starting as the Prescotts) as they move from western New York to the Pacific Coast. The all-star cast includes Carroll Baker, Lee J. Cobb, Henry Fonda, Gregory Peck, George Peppard, Robert Preston, Debbie Reynolds, James Stewart, John Wayne, and Richard Widmark. The film is narrated by Spencer Tracy. It is a big panorama of a film exploring how the West was settled with the establishment of farmsteads, towns, and businesses.

49. *The Third Man*, 1949, directed by Carol Reed: This film noir starring Joseph Cotton and Orson Welles is an unforgettable exploration of good and evil in post-war Vienna, where almost everything has a price.

50. *Giant*, 1956, directed by George Stevens: Jordan "Bick" Benedict Jr. (Rock Hudson) has inherited a sprawling Texas ranch. He marries a wealthy Marylander, Leslie Lynnton (Elizabeth Taylor), and brings her home with him to Texas. Jett Rink (James Dean) is a ranch hand who inherits a small part of the ranch. Rink discovers oil on his plot, setting in motion a dramatic conflict between the landowner aristocracy and the new rich. It is a stupendous lesson in how to handle prosperity and adversity.

APPENDIX III

The Model Company Mission Statement: Magpul Foundations

Providing innovation to the individual in the shortest time
–MAGPUL MISSION STATEMENT

THE MAGPUL FOUNDATIONS

Magpul was founded in 1999 with the intent of developing a simple device to aid in the manipulation of rifle magazines while reloading under stress. The company's name comes from this original product called the Magpul®. Over the last twenty years Magpul has continued to grow and develop using much the same mission and process with a focus on innovation, simplicity, and efficiency.

To understand Magpul, one must first understand the root ideas that form the foundation of our company culture and design philosophy. These core principles have allowed us to maintain a course true to our original mission, and help explain how and why we do the things we do.

IDEAS ARE THE EASY PART.

There is something to be said for great ideas. However, ideas are nothing more than dreams until they are realized in a form that is accessible to the marketplace. Magpul is known for its creative design solutions, and we are proud of our accomplishments in this arena not only because they are novel, but also because we have successfully turned many of our dreams into reality.

EASY IS HARD, HARD IS EASY.

Unnecessary complexity and expensive construction are the hallmarks of mediocre design. It is almost always easier to design a product that is complicated, confusing, and expensive rather than simple, intuitive, and affordable. Although it is more difficult, Magpul has chosen to take the latter of these two approaches to product development.

From the onset of every project, Magpul uses a list of mission-driven requirements to dictate design, material construction, and manufacturing methods that will be most efficient without sacrificing quality or performance. The goal of the design itself is to be both simple and intuitive. By incorporating ergonomic considerations, a proper user interface, and subtle visual and tactile features, the product itself should actually instruct the user about its operation and function. Although every Magpul product comes with clear, concise installation and usage instructions, our aim is to design products so self-explanatory that instructions become unnecessary.

FAIL SMART, FAIL OFTEN.

There is much to be learned from failure: product ideas, material properties, user interface issues, etc. The potential knowledge to be gained from a bad concept or failed execution is virtually endless. Only by pushing the limits of design, materials, and manufacturing techniques through a process of trial and error do we find true innovation. That said, failure for its own sake is foolish, and it is important to learn as much as possible from existing failures so as not to attempt to reinvent the square. This is the meaning behind "fail smart."

BUILD WHAT THEY NEED, NOT WHAT THEY WANT.

As a rule, end users are generally not designers, and are therefore limited to describing their needs in terms they know and understand. Although end user feedback is invaluable to the design process, Magpul never builds a product on the basis of simple market surveys. Instead, we study the intended mission, determine the equipment capability gap, and develop a solution based on a clearly defined set of performance-based requirements. While the end result will almost certainly not be what the user had envisioned, it will more effectively address the needs and performance capabilities they are often unable to clearly articulate or recognize from a product development perspective.

MISSION DICTATES FUNCTION, AND FUNCTION DICTATES DESIGN.

Magpul builds for the real world, so every item is built to fill a particular mission, and is designed around a unique set of cost, performance, and timeline considerations. The styling of a product follows these mission-driven parameters, and ties the functional piece into a design that can be efficiently produced.

INNOVATE OR DIE.

In the marketplace of ideas, innovation is survival. Defensible intellectual property is beneficial, but we must continually adapt our way of thinking to meet the demands of a dynamic marketplace.

PROFITS ARE NOT EVIL.

We are humbled whenever someone uses their hard-earned money to buy our products. Our products range from low-cost common applications, to high-cost specialized designs, but by pricing our products in direct relation to material development costs, they all provide value for the price. Magpul's view on profits (and money in general) is summed up in the following quote by Ayn Rand (Francisco's Money Speech, Atlas Shrugged):

"Money is the material shape of the principle that men who wish to deal with one another must deal by trade and give value for value."

BE AGGRESSIVE ENOUGH, QUICKLY ENOUGH.

The success of even the best products is contingent upon both timing and delivery. Getting a good design to market quickly and with enough force to meet consumer demand is the difference between simply breaking even or marketplace domination.

NO WINE BEFORE IT'S TIME.

Although somewhat contradictory to the previous statement, one must recognize that it is impossible to avoid "Murphy," and some products will just have to wait if they cannot meet the quality standards we have set for ourselves.

EDUCATION IS THE BEST FORM OF MARKETING.

We often get told that Magpul has slick marketing. This always makes us grin because Magpul has never used an advertising agency for our print ads or marketing materials. Everything is done in house. Our "secret" to effective marketing is simply to educate customers on the merits of our products through the internet, training classes, and instructional DVDs. Nothing slick—just honest explanations.

DO NOT BETRAY THE BRAND.

People who use Magpul products have high expectations and a great deal of trust regarding the quality and amount of thought put into every design we release. As such, all products must have the "touch" of the Magpul design team as outlined in the first part of this document. On the same note, great care must be taken not to associate the brand with any third-party product that does not adhere to the Magpul core values.

NO ONE IS USING A MAGPUL PRODUCT BECAUSE THEY HAVE TO.

When I was a Marine I routinely bought all sorts of equipment in an effort to gain a survival advantage, but most of that gear was poorly thought out and generally could not survive real life field conditions. Knowing this, I implemented a 60-day, no questions asked return policy on all Magpul products to allow the user sufficient time to field test the gear in an environment of his or her choosing. If a newly purchased piece of Magpul gear breaks or is unsuitable for the mission, send it back for a full refund. This was our policy when Magpul was founded in 1999, and it remains in effect today.

ANNOY THE ESTABLISHMENT.

I remember clearly one time at a trade show where we released some new products that were getting a lot of attention. I hid my attendee badge and walked around the show, just looking around like another nameless visitor, when I overheard someone from another company say, "I just wish Magpul would go away." Right then I knew our new products were as innovative as I suspected.

Just as America's Founding Fathers sought to promote individual rights and freedoms over those of the collective, Magpul also stands on the side of the individual. The natural enemy of the individual and innovation is the establishment and bureaucracy (which literally means "the power of the desk"). When we are annoying the establishment, we know we are effectively upholding our principles.

UNFAIR ADVANTAGE.

"If you come expecting a fair fight, you are unprepared." This common saying among military and law enforcement professionals illustrates the core values and mindset that drive everything we do at Magpul. Our customer base encompasses a broad spectrum of users; everything from hobbyists and target shooters to the most specialized and highly trained military units in the world. Regardless of the end user or their mission, our goal is to design equipment with form, fit, and function far superior to that of your "standard issue" gear. In short, we want to give you an unfair advantage.

ABOUT THE AUTHOR

Frank Miniter has floated the Amazon, run with the bulls of Pamplona, hunted everything from bear in Russia to elk with the Apache to kudu in the Kalahari, and he has fly-fished everywhere from Alaska's Kenai to Scotland's River Spey to Japan's freestone streams. Along the way he was taught to box by Floyd Patterson, spelunked into Pompey's Cave, climbed everywhere from New York's Gunks to the Rockies, and studied Kenkojuku Karate with Sensei Masakazu Takahashi. He graduated from the oldest private military academy in the United States, a place that still teaches honor and old-school gentlemanly conduct. He believes that American men need this book because too many have forgotten—or never been taught—the gentleman's code of honor.

He is the author of several books, including the bestselling *Ultimate Man's Survival Guide* and *The Politically Incorrect Guide to Hunting*, has won numerous awards for his outdoors and conservation writing, and has contributed articles to *Forbes*, *National Review*, *The Washington Times*, *The Washington Examiner*, Foxnews.com, and many other outlets. He was a senior editor at *Outdoor Life* magazine and an executive editor at *American Hunter* magazine. Currently, he is editor in chief of the NRA's political magazine, *America's 1st Freedom*.

NOTES

Introduction

1. An Phung and Chloe Melas, "Women accuse Morgan Freeman of inappropriate behavior, harassment," CNN, May 29, 2018, https://edition.cnn.com/2018/05/24/entertainment/morgan-freeman-accusations/index.html.

Rule 1

1. Audie Cornish, "Gayle King Thinks #MeToo Needs Due Process," *New York Times*, June 11, 2018, https://www.nytimes.com/2018/06/12/magazine/gayle-king-thinks-metoo-needs-due-process.html.
2. Channel 4 News, "Jordan Peterson Debate on the Gender Pay Gap, Campus Protests and Postmodernism," YouTube, January 16, 2018, https://www.youtube.com/watch?v=aMcjxSThD54&t=1319s.
3. Ibid.
4. "Read the NLRB Memo Defending Google's Firing of James Damore," Yahoo! Finance, February 16, 2018, https://finance.yahoo.com/news/read-nlrb-memo-defending-google-175157877.html.
5. "Arbitration Agreements," Workplace Fairness website, accessed May 30, 2019, https://www.workplacefairness.org/forced-arbitration-agreements#6.
6. "Sexual Harassment," U.S. Equal Employment Opportunity Commission website, accessed May 30, 2019, https://www.eeoc.gov/laws/types/sexual_harassment.cfm.
7. Gillian Tan and Katie Porzecanski, "Wall Street Rule for the #MeToo Era: Avoid Women at All Cost," Bloomberg website, December 3, 2018, https://www.bloomberg.com/news/

articles/2018-12-03/a-wall-street-rule-for-the-metoo-era-avoid-women-at-all-cost.

8. Ernest Hemingway, *A Moveable Feast* (New York: Vintage/Ebury, 2008).

9. Ibid.

10. Ernest Hemingway, *Death in the Afternoon* (P. F. Collier & Son, 1932).

Rule 2

1. Mark Twain, *More Maxims of Mark*, compiled by Merle Johnson (first edition privately printed), 1927.

2. Paul-Anthony Surdi, "How Technology Is Changing the World of Tattoos (Infographic)," TattoSchool.com, July 28, 2017, https://tattoolearning.com/how-technology-is-changing-the-world-of-tattoos/.

3. Tom Puzak, "The Rise of the 'Lumbersexual," GearJunkie, October 30, 2014, https://gearjunkie.com/the-rise-of-the-lumbersexual.

4. Mike Rowe, Facebook post, April 24, 2017, https://www.facebook.com/TheRealMikeRowe/posts/1512621355414669.

Rule 4

1. Jack Schaefer, *Shane* (Boston: Houghton Mifflin, 1949, 2001), 49.

Rule 5

1. EpicPwnTV, "Senator Barbara Boxer: 'Don't Call Me Ma'am'—General Michael Walsh," YouTube, June 18, 2009, https://www.youtube.com/watch?v=f0CprVYsG0k.

2. Susan Ricker, "Office Romance More Common Than You Think," Career Builder website, February 13, 2014, https://www.careerbuilder.com/advice/office-romance-more-common-than-you-think.

3. Emily Smith, "NBC Orders Staff to Rat Out Misbehaving Colleagues or Be Fired," PageSix.com, December 25, 2017, https://pagesix.com/2017/12/25/nbc-tightens-sexual-harassment-rules-following-matt-lauer-mess/.

4. Ibid.

5. Susan Ricker, "Office Romance more common than you think," Career Builder website, February 13, 2014, https://www.careerbuilder.com/advice office-romance-more-common-than-you-think.

6. Sheryl Sandberg, post on Facebook, February 6, 2018, https://www.facebook.com/sheryl/posts/10159854933800177.

7. Ibid.

8. Ibid.

9. Chris Morris, "Microsoft Changes Its Sexual Harassment Policies in the Wake of #MeToo," *Fortune*, December 19, 2017, http://fortune.com/2017/12/19/microsoft-changes-sexual-harassment-policies/.

10. Jordan Peterson, *12 Rules for Life: An Antidote to Chaos* (Ontario: Random House Canada, 2018).

11. Michael Kelly, *Things Worth Fighting For* (New York: Penguin Press, 2004).

12. Ibid.

Rule 6

1. *The Paris Review Interviews*, vol. I (New York: Picador, 2006), 61.

2. Joseph Cardinal Ratzinger, *Introduction to Christianity* (San Francisco: Ignatius Press, 1990), 43

3. Interview to the Press in Karachi about the execution of Bhagat Singh on March, 26, 1926, published in *Young India*, April, 2 1931.

4. Dan Bronzite, "The Hero's Journey—Mythic Structure of Joseph Campbell's Monomyth," Movie Outline, accessed June 3, 2019, http://www.movieoutline.com/articles/the-hero-journey-mythic-structure-of-joseph-campbell-monomyth.html; Stuart Voytilla, "Excerpts from *Myth and the Movies*," June 1, 2003, version, http://www.tlu.ee/~rajaleid/montaazh/Hero%27s%20Journey%20Arch.pdf.

5. Alexis Grenell, "White Women, Come Get Your People," *New York Times,* October 6, 2018, https://www.nytimes.com/2018/10/06/opinion/lisa-murkowski-susan-collins-kavanaugh.html.

6. Audrey Carlsen, Maya Salam, Claire Cain Miller, Denise Lu, Ash Ngu, Jugal K. Patel, and Zach Wichter, "#MeToo Brought Down 201 Powerful Men. Nearly Half of Their Replacements Are Women," *New York Times*, October 23, 2018, https://www.nytimes.com/interactive/2018/10/23/us/metoo-replacements.html.

7. Ibid.

8. Ibid.

9. Linda A. Bell, "Women-Led Firms and the Gender Gap in Top Executive Jobs," Social Science Research Network, July 2005, https://papers.ssrn.com/sol3/papers.cfm?abstract_id=773964.

10. Vivian Hunt, Lareina Yee, Sara Prince, and Sundiatu Dixon-Fyle, "Delivering through Diversity," McKinsey & Company, January 2018, https://www.mckinsey.com/business-functions/organization/our-insights/delivering-through-diversity.

11. Carlsen, "#MeToo Brought Down 201 Powerful Men."

12. Ibid.

13. Catalyst, Women CEOs of the S&P 500, 2017.

14. Bureau of Labor Statistics, "Table 11: Employed Persons by Detailed Occupation, Sex, Race, and Hispanic or Latino Ethnicity," *Current Population Survey, Household Data Annual Averages 2016*, 2017.

15. Bureau of Labor Statistics, "Employment Characteristics of Families Summary," Economic News Release, April 20, 2017.

16. Bureau of Labor Statistics, "Table 6: Employment Status of Mothers with Own Children under 3 Years Old by Single Year of Age of Youngest Child and Marital Status], 2014–2015 Annual Averages;" Bureau of Labor Statistics, "Table 11: Employed Persons by Detailed Occupation, Sex, Race, and Hispanic or Latino Ethnicity,"*Current Population Survey, Household Data Annual Averages 2016*, 2017.

17. Trish Joyce, "Does Healthcare Have a Gender Problem?" Health eCareers, April 24, 2018, https://www.healthecareers.com/article/healthcare-news/does-healthcare-have-a-gender-problem.

18. Carlsen, "#MeToo Brought Down 201 Powerful Men."

19. John MacQuarrie, "Dietrich Bonhoeffer," *New York Times*, June 21, 1970, https://www.nytimes.com/1970/06/21/archives/dietrich-bonhoeffer-a-life-that-meshed-with-the-rise-and-fall-of.html.

20. "Full Biography of Dietrich Bonhoeffer," The Dietrich Bonhoeffer Institute, accessed June 3, 2019, https://tdbi.org/dietrich-bonhoeffer/biography/.

21. Google Code of Conduct, accessed June 3, 2019, https://abc.xyz/investor/other/google-code-of-conduct.html.

22. The Coca-Cola Company Code of Business Conduct, accessed June 3, 2019, https://www.coca-colacompany.com/content/dam/journey/us/en/private/fileassets/pdf/our-company/2016-COBC-US-Final.pdf.

23. Hershey Code of Conduct, accessed June 3 2019, https://www.thehersheycompany.com/content/dam/corporate-us/documents/investors/code-of-conduct.pdf.

24. IBM Business Conduct Guidelines, accessed June 3, 2019, https://www.ibm.com/investor/pdf/BCG_Feb_2011_English_CE.pdf.

Rule 7

1. "Al Gore Concedes the 2000 Election," The History Place: Great Speeches Collection, December 13, 2000, http://www.historyplace.com/speeches/gore-concedes.htm.

2. Gene Siskel, "The Real Cary Grant," *Chicago Tribune*, December 7, 1986, https://www.chicagotribune.com/news/ct-xpm-1986-12-07-8604010568-story.html.

INDEX